ONE WAY THROUGH THE JUNGLE

ONE WAY THROUGH THE JUNGLE

in Borneo

Short stories from Borneo
with questions to test your knowledge

Ken Nightingale

OMF BOOKS ◇ LONDON

First published 1975

ISBN 0 85363 107 7

cover design (from a photograph by Fritz Fankhauser) and
illustrations: John Rawding

*Published by OMF BOOKS, Newington Green, London N16 9QD
with the Borneo Evangelical Mission, 58 Somerset House,
Blagrave Street, Reading, RG1 1QD*

*Made and printed in Great Britain by The Garden City Press Limited,
Letchworth, Hertfordshire SG6 1JS*

JESUS said:
'I am
THE WAY
and
THE TRUTH
and
THE LIFE . . .'

John 14.6

CONTENTS

FOREWORD

by Michael Griffiths, General Director, Overseas Missionary Fellowship.

In view of the integration in the field between the Overseas Missionary Fellowship and the Borneo Evangelical Mission, it gives me special pleasure to introduce to readers this book about tribal work in northern Borneo.

Ken Nightingale has given us a book which is different. He introduces us to the astonishing variety of a world that still exists alongside our own, beyond the fringes of our technocratic civilization. It is a world of spirits and sacrifices, of monkeys and orang-utans, of witchdoctors and head hunters' skulls, of betel-nut and rice-beer, of pigs and pythons, crocodiles and cobras.

The short chapters give us a realistic picture of life in modern Borneo as we fly over the jungle in aeroplanes and helicopters and travel along the rivers in canoes.

The questions that conclude each chapter help us to see that missionaries must grapple with problems of life and death, of funerals and feasts, which our own cultural experience may not help us to answer, but which we find that the Bible will.

Many missionaries today work in the great cities of the Third World, but the toughest challenge, requiring even greater dedication, is that of identifying with the more neglected and deprived societies of mankind. The simpler the life of the people and the more unlike the culture from which the missionaries come, the bigger is the imaginative leap the missionary has to take to cross the cultural gap, in order to understand such a different culture and identify with it. We note too that the impact of the big city is felt even here in drawing young people away from the long-houses in the jungle.

To those who feel that 'people are all right as they are' without interference from missionaries, this book may make them think again. What we find is not the noble savage or happy heathen living in primaeval splendour. It is a world of fear of evil spirits and taboos, malnutrition and sickness. If this is puzzling to some readers, let it be appreciated that these people have little doubt about the reality of the supernatural and conflict with the powers of darkness. To some in the West the ideas of exorcism and the occult have a certain bizarre fascination, because of their very unfamiliarity. To those who live permanently where they are the frightening commonplace of daily living, the situation is very different.

If we doubt whether there are any spiritual forces hostile to men and ranged against us, we may end up doubting also whether there are spiritual forces ranged on our side. In the jungle of Borneo the battle is joined, as we see missionaries and Bornean Christians together seeking to deliver others from the terror of demons. The heroes and heroines of this book are not so much the missionaries, but their national brethren, themselves set free from the service of the spirits, and yet still in everyday contact with those who still serve them. After what might seem (to those who have never faced it personally), an over-preoccupation with the supernatural conflict, we are amused at the missionary scared at things which go bump in the night!

Missionaries are busy people. Most of them think about writing a book at some time, and some of them have an unfinished manuscript in their baggage. Often that manuscript never sees the light of day or fails to survive the discouragement of a first refusal. We are most grateful therefore to Ken Nightingale for persisting and giving us such a realistic picture.

The author is an Australian, an accountant by training, who served with the British Navy during the second world war in northern waters and Russia. (His cousin Peter works among tribal people in North Thailand.) He is married with three children and has worked in Borneo since 1952.

Singapore, 1975

EARLY WORDS

How do tribesfolk tick over? What are their hopes and fears? And the missionaries who work among them; are they a special breed of spiritual giant? How do missionaries and tribal Christians interact in the progress of the Good News? If these are some of your questions, I hope that you will be helped by these short stories.

You may think that some of them are strange but they are chosen not because of any strangeness they may appear to have, but rather because they portray things typical of missionary work among the tribes of Borneo.

Borneo is a rugged land whose poor communications and proliferation of languages have both contrived to give the Gospel a rough passage. Yet, in spite of this, the Good News has taken root in many tribal villages. And more, lively groups are also springing up in the towns.

The stories are true. However, as a few of them were written up from notes taken on the wing, I have had to provide a little background detail here and there from my knowledge of the situation. I do apologize if I have misread the signals at any point.

All the names of the people involved have been changed, as also have village names. The aim of the stories is not to lionize any person or persons, for we are all still in process, creatures of change, to be presented in *that day* perfect in Christ Jesus. The idea of the book is to give you a general picture of the way things happen in this part of the world and how people function in the missionary context.

A friend of mine once received a photo sent to him by an acquaintance. On the back of it was the caption: 'Me preaching'! Although most of these stories are taken from my own experience, lots of other people, both missionary brethren and Bornean, come into the history of them and I do thankfully acknowledge their part in the teamwork.

I personally have had very little close-up experience of dealing with the demon-possessed. It is certainly a frightening realm in which one has to move most carefully and prayerfully.

There has been the awareness, intense at times, of the spiritual conflict. This warfare is relentless. And it is directed against the Christian and especially anyone who comes in Christ's name to upset the satanic *status quo*. The danger for me has been in getting my eyes on people and seeming *human* opposition when the Scriptures remind us so clearly that '... we are not fighting against people ... but ... mighty satanic beings and ... huge numbers of wicked spirits in the spirit world' (Ephesians 6.12). Only Christ can deal with those beings and set the people free, because of His complete victory over the satanic hosts. We go in His strong name.

I would underline that this does not come from someone who considers he's arrived. God knows. I feel more of a learner now than when I arrived in Borneo in 1952. You know how it is when some of us arrive on the field, we want to do all the talking and none of the listening! After the Lausanne Congress, 1974, an Asian bishop wrote, '... humility is required in our approach to the non-Christian world. This may well result in a new type of missionary who is willing to go as a *learner* rather than an expert.'

This book was not written for the experts. But, if it leads you to search out the experts, well and good. The list at the end, of books I have read, may be of help. One book that has been of particular help to me in thinking about animistic people is J. Warneck's *The Living Christ and Dying Heathenism*. I'm sure that many more of his thoughts and assessments have crept into my stories than I have acknowledged. I consider this book to be a classic in its field.

The Talkback

If you wish to settle just for the stories, that's fine. But for folk wishing to play it serious, such as those in discussion groups, etc, the *Talkback* is offered. These talkback questions occur at the end of each chapter and usually relate to themes inherent in the stories. Many of the questions are presented from a 'you be the missionary' angle. I know that it would have helped me a lot in my missionary life to have faced some of these questions *before* arriving on the field.

I have tried to avoid hypothetical talkback. My choice of questions was not with the technical man in mind but rather to encourage ordinary folk in some missionary thinking. For the best use of the talkback in a discussion group, it would be good if each member had a copy of the book and could do a little homework before the group comes together. Such preparation is essential at least to the group leader if the discussion is to be well directed and not develop into an untidy free-for-all. The Scripture texts given are only suggestions to get you started. I hope you will make the Scriptures central in your studies and trust the Holy Spirit to lead you through to right conclusions.

A prayer to guide you, from a very wise man :

'Open my eyes to see wonderful things in your Word. I am but a pilgrim here on earth : how I need a map—and your commands are my chart and guide' (Psalm 119.18–19).

KEN NIGHTINGALE,
Lawas, Sarawak.

WHERE ON EARTH IS BORNEO?

Borneo is an island, the third largest in the world. It is in South-east Asia and lies firmly planted between Peninsular Malaysia and the Philippines. By what route would you fly there from your country?

BORNEO AND S.E. ASIA

If you like comparisons, Borneo is larger than the whole of France: about 800 miles long and 600 miles across at its widest point.

Being right on the equator, this is a sunny island and one of the best-watered countries in the world—that's if you like lots of water! Its 100–200 inches of rain annually really make the rivers flow. Many of them come hurtling down via steep gorges and dangerous rapids from the mountains. Yet, some Bornean tribesfolk are thankful for their rivers that act as roads, winding and sometimes rapid-strewn, linking them to other villages and coastal towns.

We said earlier that this is a rugged country to travel in. Apart from the coastal highways, few are the roads that stretch into the mountainous interior. This is why you'll need aircraft in Borneo. Without them, communications, poor at any time, would be hopelessly incomplete. Aircraft have been used in missionary work for the past 24 years and have had a lot to do with the opening up of the hinterland to the Good News.

Borneo is not heavily peopled. It can only boast a population of $4\frac{1}{2}$ million, nearly 2 million of whom live in the north to north-western quarter which is now called East Malaysia. (See map). The 300,000-strong Iban tribe is the largest tribal group, followed by the Kadazan. The Chinese and Malays live in the coastal regions in good numbers.

Many of the tribesfolk are longhouse dwellers who live in communities of up to 100 families, sharing a common life under an elected headman and village elders. The majority of them are still animists (spirit worshippers) whilst the Malays are Islamic and the Chinese largely Buddhist.

How did Borneo get on the map? The history books give us evidence of the Chinese trading with this country from the 6th and 7th centuries AD, when their big junks came loaded with such things as pottery and hardware. If we'd read the ships' manifests for the return journey we'd possibly have seen listed such things as hornbill, ivory, beeswax, rhinocerous horn, camphor canes and bezoar stones ('monkey gall-stones').

Europeans first came on the scene in the 16th century and opened up some lively arteries of trade. James Brooke, the British adventurer, first appeared in the area in 1839 and a little later became the State of Sarawak's first white rajah, beginning an era of British influence. The first missionary, an Anglican by the name of the Rev. F. T. McDougall, arrived in Sarawak's capital, Kuching, in 1848. The British colonies of Sarawak and Sabah (previously North Borneo) became federated states of Malaysia in 1963, and are together known as East Malaysia.

Borneo is a land of many languages. In a number of areas you could change language every few miles. About

. .

181 different tribes or groups have been recorded in Sarawak alone. This has meant loads of work for the few Bible translators who have been hard at it putting the Word of God into some of the languages. The folk here love their own language just as you love yours. A gracious old Chinese gentleman, in speaking about the expected joys of heaven remarked, 'And won't it be grand there, no more difficulty understanding each other. We'll all speak the same language. And that language will be Chinese!'

Borneo is a beautiful country, but not an unspoiled garden of Eden. It's true, there is so much natural beauty to gladden the heart. But when we turn to the natural religions, the scene is different. We find awful distortion and ugliness. The imagination of heathenism has run riot. The grotesque and often obscene idols of animism will repel you, and the hideous images of Buddhism will cause you to wonder what has possessed men to produce and bow down to such weird and repulsive objects. Animism (fear and worship of spirits) is the dominant tribal religion.

Pagans never greet each other by saying : 'god be with you', or 'god bless you.' On the contrary, their gods are thought of as objects of remoteness and often of dread, not of endearment or whose company is delighted in.

What a contrast to the true God of love and beauty that we know, who invites fellowship with His children.

The name *Borneo* is used in this book in a loosely descriptive way. The states of Sarawak and Sabah, from which these stories come, are situated in the northern and north-western sectors of the island of Borneo. Many of the customs referred to apply widely throughout the whole of the island.

The stories relate to the work of the Borneo Evangelical Mission (BEM) which began work in Sarawak in 1928. It is now working alongside a young and active indigenous church called The Evangelical Church of Borneo. On January 1st, 1975, the BEM became affiliated to the Overseas Missionary Fellowship (OMF).

HUNTER'S PRIZE

*Jali soon got busy with his small stripping knife, carving
up the monkey into small pieces ... I smiled at the way he
performed over the animal, like a skilled surgeon demonstrating anatomy to a willing student. He held up one part
after another for my benefit ...*

'And we eat all these parts,' he said. 'They are all good.'
I cringed and tried to look the other way ...

Take One Monkey ... 1

1 Take One Monkey

'Come on Jali, get your gun. Let's go hunting.'

What was I saying? Me, on a hunt with Jali? I'd another think coming.

Jali was a good hunter and, what was more, he was one of the favoured few of his tribe who had a shotgun. We were living together in a little hut at the edge of the river not far from a big pagan village which we will call Long Tering. We had been trying for a long time to contact the folk there with the Good News but we were having little success.

What did they think of Christ? Not very much at this stage. If they thought of Him at all it was to ask themselves how he related to their tireless struggle for food, for shelter and for protection from the evil spirits that they felt were threatening their very existence. How did Christ relate to these basic things, they wondered?

It would have been an impudence to expect them to feed us, for they were poor and hungry. They had had to abandon some of their rice farms through bad omens, and often their witchdoctors forbade them to go out hunting.

That is why Jali and I set up for ourselves. We lived on some rice that we had brought with us, plus whatever we could shoot or gather. We had had some nice fern tips and some tapioca. But now we were feeling like something more substantial.

'Are you ready, Jali?' I called.

Jali stuck a few cartridges into his belt and we set off. His jungle knife was at his side. It was a golden morning. I think Jali prayed, asking God to give us something for our search and to watch over us. It was his normal practice. Very soon we left the track that followed the river and branched off into some primary forest growth.

Then, the jungle began to thicken and the climbing became more difficult, so much so that I was beginning to review my part in this outing. Was I really necessary on this journey? Was it the pace Jali was setting? Whatever

it was, my heart was pounding. Jali kept turning round
and proffering little titbits of encouragement as he surveyed
my pitiful bid for survival, for that was what it was turning
into. I soon concluded that he would be happier without
his doubtful escort. My part in the hunt was developing
into little more than a hunt for Jali.

'Press on, Jali. I'll see you back at the hut', I called,
turning for home.

Jali waved his approval and soon disappeared into the
green city. If I knew Jali, he'd not return empty-handed.

On my way back, I glanced over at the pagan village
across the river, a cluster of old leaf-roofed longhouses,
built close together for collective security and standing high
off the ground in a kind of proud defiance. But there were
folk there with whom we longed to talk. I was glad to get
back to our hut to refresh my failing spirits with a little
coffee.

At about four that afternoon, I heard a shot resound
through the jungle from the area where I had left Jali.
He must be coming back, I thought, and has seen something nearer base. After a while there was another shot and
then a third and a fourth. Jali must be after something
evasive or hard to bring down. All kinds of surmises were
running through my mind when the man himself suddenly
appeared at the door, his legs scratched and his feet
bleeding from leech bites.

'Did you hear the shots?' he asked.

'Yes, I did, but where's the animal?'

'I've shot a large monkey high up in a tree, but I can't
dislodge him', he replied.

'Well, what are you going to do?' I asked, appealingly.

'Don't worry', he said. 'I've prayed to God and asked
Him to send a wind tonight to blow him down. And I'll go
back in the morning and pick him up off the ground.'

I soon had a meal ready for Jali as he was famished,
and as our little wick lamp was not much to read by we
turned in to bed, hoping that the next day might bring us
some answered prayer and some meat to improve our diet.

HUNTER'S REWARD

I awoke next morning to find Jali's sleeping mat vacant.
He was up and away before the sun rose, as his aim was to
get the meat before a jungle animal did. Also, the sun on it
would soon turn it bad. Jali was not a child of the jungle
for nothing.

At about eight that morning, as the sun was peeping over
the high trees nearby, Jali came bounding up the steps with
the monkey strapped like a baby to his back.

'God has been good to us', he said. 'This is a young man
monkey—plenty of good meat and rich fat.'

Jali soon got busy with his small stripping knife, carving
up the monkey into small pieces suitable for putting on a
skewer for smoking over our wood fire. He looked in vain
for any sign of a bezoar stone. These things, sometimes
referred to as gall-stones, are occasionally found in the
alimentary organs of certain animals. Those from monkeys
are dark brown in colour, smooth as a pebble and sometimes as large as a pheasant's egg. The tribesfolk regard
them as a great prize and sell them to the Chinese who pay
big prices for them as an ingredient in their traditional
medicine.

I smiled at the way Jali performed over the animal, like
a skilled surgeon demonstrating anatomy to a willing
student. He held up one part after another for my benefit,
stating the native names for the various parts of the monkey's abdominal equipment.

'And we eat all these parts', he said. 'They are all good.'

I cringed and tried to look the other way.

'Yes, Jali, I'm sure they are all good. You shall have
them all', I answered. I could take the meat but not the
other delicacies. Then, he severed the head with rare precision and to my dismay placed it carefully above the
fireplace.

'The brain too', he continued. 'It will be delicious after
it has matured over the fire for a few days.'

It was not the maturing process that later bothered me,
but rather the skull's contemptuous, half-closed eyes that
peered down upon us from the fireplace for the next three

days. Jali then cracked it open like a walnut and ate the brain with appropriate relish.

The way Jali got that monkey touched my heart. I have always admired the simple faith of Jali's jungle people. They have helped me become more simple in my own faith and to trust the Lord more about everyday things.

Before we opened our sleeping mats that night, we thanked our Heavenly Father for putting some food into our pot. It encouraged us. He was still there caring for us, despite the indifference of the Long Tering folk over the river.

But their time would come. Surely, it would come soon.

Guidelines

God the giver
'The eyes of all mankind look up to you for help; you give them their food as they need it' (Psalm 145.15, Living Bible).

Sowing the seed
'They that sow in tears shall reap in joy' (Psalm 126.5 AV).

Talkback

1 *No meat?* If Jali had got no meat and asked you as the missionary whether God had heard his prayer, how would you have answered him? (Isaiah 30.18; Lamentations 3.25–26; Matthew 18.19; Luke 18.1.)

2 *Better crops?* Should we have told these poverty-stricken pagan people that the Christian Way could give them better crops? (Matthew 6.25–33; John 6.25–35; Philippians 4.19.)

3 *Countdown* Do you think that God has a particular time for working in pagan hearts? (Mark 1.15; Luke 19.41–44; Acts 16.7, 9–10; 2 Corinthians 6.2; Galatians 4.4–5.)

4 *Prayer* How big a factor is prayer in bringing pagan people to Christ? (Psalm 2.8; Matthew 18.19–20; Ephesians 6.19; Colossians 4.3.)

A time to live

> 'There is a right time for everything :
> A time to be born, a time to die;
> A time to plant;
> A time to harvest'
> (Ecclesiastes 3.1, 2 Living Bible.)

BLOOD AND THE SPIRITS

*'The spirits want more blood. More blood, do you under-
stand? You must restrict yourselves more. Discipline, that's
the thing . . .'*

*A heart-rending silence followed. Was this all that
Deacon Lenjau had to offer?*

*He let the effect of his words sink in before pouring in
the oil . . . 'Yes, more blood's the thing—or perhaps you'd
like to take a little advice from an old friend:*

*'My brothers, you can dispense with this devilish
madness . . .'*

The Orang-Utan's Head . . . 2

The Orang-Utan's Head

'This is no ordinary animal', declared the witchdoctors. 'This is a gift to us from the spirits.' They immediately placed a taboo on the longhouse. No one was to leave. No visitors were allowed. The kindness of the spirits had to be acknowledged with due ritual.

The orang-utan was considered an animal of special breed. It looked so human and the folk of this tribal village had longed to lay their hands on one. Think of the prestige for a man if he could track one down, shoot it and bring it to the longhouse!

On this day a hunter was rewarded. He arrived home with an orang-utan strapped to his back, and proudly walked the full length of the longhouse verandah to show it off. He had shot it down from a high tree. Tell-tale fruit skins and chewed seeds on the ground had given away its secret feeding place. It didn't take much marksmanship to bring down such a large quarry to earth.

The village children were delighted, to say nothing of their elders. They nudged it, fluffed up its fur and pulled its beard, calling it 'old grandfather.'

For a day or two the folk fêted the body of the orang-utan, stroking it and parading it around with glee, until the day of the big celebration when the severing of the head took place. The head—that was the prize. They already had several sheaves of smoke-blackened human skulls festooning the longhouse verandah. This would make a precious addition. In both man and beast the soul-stuff was found in abundance in the head, they believed.

The old men still revelled in blood-curdling accounts of the taking of enemy skulls. Such stories terrified the children, especially when told at night. They could see enemy presences in the night illuminations of every fire-fly. Head-hunting days were times of terror when no one was really safe outside the stockades of his own village. But head-hunting was forbidden now; that was some comfort.

The head of the orang-utan would be a good substitute

for a human head, the witchdoctors said. The village desperately needed new spirit, some luck; something to break the run of ill-fortune, bad crops, sickness and untimely death that had been bursting out at every seam.

Our boat arrives

Our longboat pulled into the bank at this village of Long Tering bringing us on another visit soon after their orang-utan haul. Pigs, nosing for roots in the leafy mud, scampered off at our arrival. One stayed there and sniffed defiantly at us. Very soon a handful of folk were down at our boat asking for medicine.

'There's still much sickness about', they said.

'Bad luck', remarked an old philosopher.

'But hasn't your luck changed lately?' asked Deacon Lenjau, one of our team, making subtle reference to their recent prize.

'Bah!' replied one of the women as she spat impatiently on the ground. 'Why don't you come up into the longhouse?'

The celebrations surrounding the orang-utan were all over, but the stench of stale beer and rotting rice husk still hovered around the island of mud that fronted the longhouse. We were quickly offered hospitality. A tin containing ready-made betel-nut wads was pushed in front of us as a sign of their welcome.

If you want your pulse quickened or a little dutch courage, then a wad of betel-nut is the thing. But, if you are a novice you should go warily, for your tongue will burn and your legs may go wobbly as your mouth fills with the red saliva. However, the discomfort may help you forget your other troubles for a while. But only for a while if you'd lived at Long Tering, for I have rarely seen a people with more self-inflicted wounds; wounds of a cruel, Satanic bondage.

We found that some of the folk were getting tired of the hazy half-answers to their questions which the witchdoctors were offering. It was true, they did believe that there was a beneficent Supreme Being, a good spirit way out there, but he was too distant to be of much help, they thought.

It was significant that the witchdoctors were now old men, all of them, stoical guardians of traditions handed down to them from a darker age. Could we hope that the people were just waiting for an opportunity to make a break to the Christian faith?

Many missionary tears had been shed over this village, for we had been calling here for several years, most times just to sow a seed of compassion, but sowing in hope.

THE SPIRITS WANT MORE BLOOD

Deacon Lenjau was indeed a puzzle to them. He was one of their own tribe from another village, yet he looked as if he'd not a care in the world. Folk questioned him: 'How come you're a Christian? You must have powerful protection. Aren't you scared that one day the spirits will get even with you for breaking faith?'

They could understand a white skin being a Christian, but this tribal man—well, all brown skins were animists like themselves. Wasn't it tempting the gods to break away from the traditions of the fathers? And what was more, this man seemed to be on a different tack. In all his visits he had said nothing about how to become rich or acquire many children, but always spoke about 'the Good One' and 'the clean life.' Mysterious, very mysterious, but intriguing!

Lenjau sat there and smiled. He knew of their life and their long and futile service to the spirits. He returned their banter by inviting them to talk of their felicity in their present heathen state.

Out came the stories of demon possessions, a moonlight flight for fear of the spirits, the deaths, the taboos and poor crops. They looked to him for a response.

'Of course, of course', he replied. 'You have spoken well; your words are true, every one. But, it becomes obvious to me that this distress of yours is increasing because you are not hitting the sacrifices hard enough. The spirits want more blood. More blood, do you understand? You must restrict yourselves more. Discipline, that's the thing. You've just got to take the spirits more seriously.' A heart-rending silence followed. Was this all that Deacon Lenjau had to offer?

He let the effect of his words sink in before pouring in the oil.

'Yes, more blood's the thing—or perhaps you'd like to take a little advice from an old friend. My brothers', Lenjau went on, straightening himself as he went to the point, 'you can dispense with this devilish madness as I did. You can be free of it all. Jesus Christ is stronger than Satan. He can be your Good Leader if you'll only make the break.'

More silence. If only we could have read their thoughts, the struggles going on, the secret longings. One man found a crack in the floor boards and spat, accurately. It relieved the tension.

'Sir', said another, turning to me, 'Did you bring any medicine for a sick stomach?'

Guidelines

Shepherdless sheep
'As he saw the crowds, his heart was filled with pity for them, because they were worried and helpless, like sheep without a shepherd' (Matthew 9.36 TEV).

Compassion
'Remember those who are suffering, as though you were suffering as they are' (Hebrews 13.3b TEV).

Talkback

1 *Authority* By what authority does the missionary go to a pagan longhouse and bid the folk turn to a drastically new concept of life? (Matthew 24.14; 28.19–20; Acts 1.8.)
2 *Supreme Being* Has the Bible anything to say about the innate knowledge that these pagan people had of a

Supreme Being? (John 1.8–9; Acts 17.26–30; Romans
1.19–20; 2.15.)

3 *Hopeless?* What Scriptures help us not to give up on
people who seem impossible? (Genesis 18.23–33; Psalm
126.5; Hebrews 12.1–3; James 5.11; 2 Peter 3.9.)

4 *Hospitality* If you were offered a wad of betel-nut or
a mug of rice beer at this village, would you take it? What
factors would govern your response? (1 Corinthians 8.9–13;
Romans 14.15–17.)

The important thing

'Don't do anything that will cause criticism against yourself
even though you know that what you do is right. For, after
all, the important thing for us as Christians is not what we
eat or drink but stirring up goodness and peace and joy
from the Holy Spirit' (Romans 14.16–17 Living Bible).

VAIN OFFERING

Every vestige of trust that Bulan had in medicine men was smashed that day when she returned unhealed from the place of the dead. She had killed the pig and offered its blood as prescribed, and what had happened? Precisely nothing! Bulan spat ... as she thought about it.

'More waste of blood and effort', she screeched. The pain was digging its teeth in. 'We must call the Christians ... If their God can heal me, then the Christians have the power ...'

The Big Burn ... 3

3 The Big Burn

'The spirits are torturing me', gasped Bulan as she came in from the longhouse verandah and sank down on to her sleeping mat.

She had been plagued of late with this pain in her left arm. It had hung limp at her side for quite a while. Any attempt to lift it almost made her scream. She had taken her complaint to the medicine men and they had tried in vain to find a reason for it. How had she offended the spirits? they asked. What had she done? Whom had she been with that could have blighted her life with an evil spell? The sickness must have a reason behind it. Sicknesses didn't just happen!

They had performed all kinds of magic art over her and she had paid them dearly : cloth, money, jungle knives; but all to no avail. Finally, one of them felt that he really did have the answer to her malady. 'The spirits of the dead have been offended. You must take a pig to the graveyard and make an offering of its blood. Then the sickness will be taken from you.'

BULAN'S DESPAIR
Every remaining vestige of trust that Bulan had in medicine men was smashed that day when she returned unhealed from the place of the dead. She had killed the pig and offered its blood as prescribed and what had happened? Precisely nothing! Bulan spat on the ground as she thought of it.

'More waste of blood and effort', she screeched. The pain was digging its teeth in. 'We must call the Christians. Yes, call the Christians. If their God can heal me then the Christians have the power. Christians we must become !'

The Christians were called at Bulan's word. She was a woman of breeding and spoke with authority in the village.

Deacon Madang screwed up his eyes to adjust them to

the darkness as he entered Bulan's shuttered room. 'Bulan, are you there?' a villager called as he took Madang in.

'Of course I'm here. Where else would I be?' replied Bulan testily from her mat in the corner. 'Can't move; I'm sick. Finished. I ask your pity, Madang, because I want your God to heal me.' She then rehearsed the marathon of fruitless journeys to medicine men, of the pigs sacrificed and money wasted. And what had she got in return?

'Say no more. I know it all', replied Madang, a man who in his pagan days had been through the senseless excursion of stratagems to try and appease or outwit the spirits of sickness and evil.

'Now, let us pray and tell our Big Father all about it. He cares for you.' Bulan winced as she tried to sit up. Eventually she made it. She knew that Christians closed their eyes when they prayed. She followed suit.

'O Father who pities poor people and has compassion on those who are weak', she heard Madang say. 'Yes, that's me', Bulan thought. 'Poor, wretched, weak, He knows all about me.' The pleading in Madang's voice and the friend-to-friend way he talked with his Big Father really hit home with her. He seemed to have a direct line. 'Something must come of this', she thought.

'Now, you just think about our Big Father. I've asked Him to do the best thing for you', said Madang. 'Whatever happens now will be from Him. Lie down now and take your rest.' And sleep Bulan did.

THE CHRISTIANS' GOD HEALS

Folk were staggered to see her bustling around the next morning and using her 'bad' arm. She had been healed. Before the first trills of the magpie robin she was up and about, kindling the fire and cooking rice for her visitors. Never had the folk seen the like of it. 'Our Big Father has pitied her', said Madang. 'He has power to do these things.'

This was the first of several remarkable healings that occurred at Long Tering after prayers to the Christians' God. Things like this were stubborn arguments for His power. Following Bulan's healing, a big village meeting was called.

'All right then', said the headman, summing up the night's discussion as to whether the village wanted to turn to the Christian way or stick with the old custom. 'I take it that you want to say farewell to the old way and call Madang back here to teach us about his Big Father?'

'Well, am I right?'

'Ah, that's it', called one and then another, until a crescendo of approval ran throughout the whole gathering. It had been a hard night for a couple of the old witch-doctors who had been defending their cause like a bear with whelps.

A tingle of excitement ran through the village. The Christians had life, a hymnbook, they could read and sing and do things. Expectation bristled, especially among the young. We could sense it as our boat pulled in once more to this village of Long Tering, and led by Madang and Lisa we made our way up the brown river bank to this big longhouse that had been resistant for so long. We then began introducing the folk to the Christian faith.

What a day for them as they witnessed the closing cere-mony to centuries of pagan darkness among them and the taking on of a whole new way of life with a living, loving Father right at its centre; a God and a Saviour.

THE CLEAN-OUT

'Are you sure that you have nothing else in this room that belongs to your old custom?' enquired Madang. 'If you hide it, remember, our God will not be pleased. He will not share His kingdom with the devil.'

We moved from room to room, praying in each one and teaching the folk about Jesus' power over Satan. We asked the occupants to scour the place for every trace of the old custom that belonged to the devil. We knew only too well what happens to folk who hold back. Confusion reigns.

Out came the fetishes, charm stones, little bottles of coloured liquid, dried animal entrails and snail shells in which their spirits would hide when it thundered. Our collecting basket was fast becoming full. A strange array indeed, laced with all manner of sacred leaves and feathers dipped in blood. Every room was committed into the hands of our Big Father. We asked Him to look after them now and teach them the rules of His Kingdom.

'And now, what about the heads?' asked Lisa as we came out on to the longhouse verandah where a cluster of grimy skulls leered down at us from the rafters.

'You go up for them; we're scared', the men replied. Lisa encouraged them to take a step of trust in the Lord. In a flash, one of the young men scaled up to the rafters and severed the rattan twine, sending the sheaf of skulls crashing to the floor. Some stray hens raced for cover.

The last room visited was that of the village witch. She was terrified and the elders asked strong prayer for her.

As we entered her room she pointed with her chin towards a shelf projecting outside. On it were some betel-nut and egg offerings to the mountain spirit whom she said was a frequent caller. No, he didn't actually remove the betel-nut wads and the eggs. He took the spirit of them when he came down from his mountain hide-out at night. Folk had sometimes seen him; a giant figure with spear in hand. His voice was the thunder.

Now he was about to be robbed of his food. The witch trembled as the food was taken in. She stumblingly followed our strong pleas to the Lord Jesus to save and protect her.

Outside, a number of egg offerings were collected from their forked-stick holders and consigned to the big basket. It had a voracious appetite. Two strong men then hauled it along to an open spot where, surrounded by a group of witnesses, a pyre was made and a royal bonfire reduced the whole ungodly muster to ashes.

As we gathered the folk together for a parting word, we asked them not to look back. The old bird calls, animal noises and thunderings would occur just the same. Sickness and death would still come unbidden. And they would still have the same next-door neighbour! But the significance of all these things would now be changed.

'You now have a Big Father and His Son Jesus to help

you. Speak to them often', we urged. Already, we could see that they were getting acquainted. My biggest concern was, where were we going to get a pastor to live with them and nurture them in the ways of the Lord?

Guidelines

Our task
'... to open their eyes, that they may turn from darkness to light and from the power of Satan to God, that they may receive forgiveness of sins and a place among those who are sanctified by faith in me' (Acts 26.18 RSV).

A simple promise
'Every one who calls upon the name of the Lord will be saved' (Romans 10.13 RSV).

Talkback

1 *Caution* Do you think we should look with suspicion on everything of pagan culture? (1 Thessalonians 5.21–23.)
2 *Clean-out* Is it a good idea for the evangelists to gather and throw out the pagan paraphernalia, or should they urge the people to do it themselves? (Deuteronomy 7.5; Acts 19.17–20; Mark 8.34–38; Hebrews 11.6.)
3 *Faith* How important is it that we give expression to our faith? (James 2.14–17; Hebrews 11.6ff.)
4 *Drunk* What teaching would you give, as the missionary, if some of the folk in this village constantly appeared at your services drunk? (Ezekiel 36.25–27; Mark 1.15; 1 Corinthians 6.9–11; 2 Corinthians 5.17–18.)

Christ for every day

'And now just as you trusted Christ to save you, trust him, too, for each day's problems; live in vital union with him' (Colossians 2.6 Living Bible).

PAGAN TREASURES

We gathered up Apui's old, pagan treasures and prepared to take them to the river.

'Where are you going with those?' Apui asked with some concern.

'Why, we're taking them to the river. You don't want them any more, do you?'

'No ... but could you take them somewhere else? If you throw them into the river, the devil will send us a flood tomorrow.'

'Have no fear, Apui. Jesus is greater than Satan.'

Apui grunted a degree of understanding.

The Man Who Came in from the Edge ... 4

4   The Man Who Came in from the Edge

'It's no use just looking at the gate. You've got to go through it.'

'Who? Me? Me, go through that gate? Well, I suppose he's right. I've never been through that little gate he's talking about. I've always stood back just looking at it, like he says. And if I stay where I am I'll get carried along that broad way to destruction.' Apui, the headman, was talking to himself.

This encounter occurred in the same longhouse of Long Tering some six years after their turning to the Lord. Some had held back, including the old headman himself. That is why I made a particular point of pressing the matter of entering the straight gate that Jesus referred to in Matthew 7. The big picture I was using of The Two Ways, the way of life through the little gate and the way of destruction via the broad way, graphically pressed home the truth.

I could see the old headman sitting out on the edge of the longhouse crowd on that humid February evening.

'Don't be like the folk of Noah's day who watched the building of the ark for 120 years but didn't enter it. They looked at it but perished outside in the flood', I continued.

'Yes, the man's right. He's talking about me', the headman said to himself. 'My hurt pride has kept me on the outside just like I am now, sitting on the edge of this meeting.'

In the morning he was up early and we found him at daybreak waiting at the edge of our sleeping mats. He wanted to talk and we let him.

'When you came here six years ago all my people said they wanted to follow the Lord. I was angry because my heart was still a little bit with the devil. I wanted them to humour me and entice me to join them in turning to the Lord. But they didn't. They had no respect for my age or position. I was angry and said in my heart, "I'll just be an onlooker at this Way, but my heart will still be in the devil's camp".'

He was a fine warrior-type of man. I could well imagine him returning as victor from a headhunt. He shuffled and uncrossed his long legs as he ended his story.

'But last night that story hit me hard. I want to enter that gate. Will you pray for me?'

'That's wonderful news, Apui', I said. 'You are making a very wise choice. Jesus wants you to have life and not to be destroyed by the devil's power. But tell me, have you any of Satan's medicines or secret charms hidden away? They must all come out. You can't get through that narrow gate with them. There just isn't room.'

The old man glanced up and down again quickly. He seemed unsettled for some reason or other. 'No', he replied, 'I haven't got anything like that any more.'

These charms. How hard to make the break. Some of them were inherited from ancestors and had sentimental value as well as supernatural power. They were not only their protection but a sacred inheritance. For a man to lose his charms meant exposing him and his family to grave risks, unless of course he had some better protection. No wonder folk were reluctant to part with them.

But now, could we hope that Apui was ready to take Jesus as his protection? As his Saviour?

'We'll pray then, Apui, if you are really sure that you are ready and are holding nothing back.'

HIDDEN 'TREASURE'
'Just a minute', Apui interrupted, jumping up abruptly and reaching for an old tin. He brought it down quickly on to the mat and began searching inside it. He came out with a small, rusty container. This he opened with great deliberation, spilling its contents out on to the floor. Lying before us was an array of small medicine phials, round charm-stones and sacred parts of animal intestines.

We sat there open-mouthed. 'Anything else, Apui?' I asked, hardly able to believe my eyes. 'Are you really sure there is not one other devil-thing that you have secreted away?'

'Nothing, nothing!'

'All right then, let us all pray.'

Apui said that he was now trusting fully in Jesus. After a little chat together and a drink of coffee served by Apui's gracious wife, we gathered up his old, pagan treasures and prepared to take them down to the river.

'Where are you going with those?' Apui asked with some concern.

'Why, we're taking them to the river. You don't want them any more, do you?'

'No', said Apui. 'But could you take them somewhere else? You see, if you throw them into the river, the devil will take revenge and send us a flood tomorrow.'

'Have no fear, Apui. Jesus is greater than Satan. You will see His power in this. We will throw them into the river and ask Him to spare us from all evil', we assured him.

Apui grunted a degree of understanding.

We left the village next day. The river was beautifully low and clear. We hoped that Apui got the message.

Guidelines

Come in

Jesus said, 'I am the door; if anyone enters by me, he will be saved . . .' (John 10.9 RSV).

Talkback

1 *Hell*   Apui was disturbed by the flames of hell in the picture. Is such imagery true to what Christ taught about the final judgement of folk who reject Him? (Matthew 25.41; Luke 16.22–24.)

2 *Help*   What did Christ do to keep people out of hell?

(Isaiah 53.3–6; Matthew 27.27–37; Luke 9.22; Hebrews 13.12; 1 Peter 3.18.)

3 *Fear* How wholesome is fear as an emotion in relation to God? (Exodus 20.20; Proverbs 14.27; Psalm 111.10; Revelation 15.2–4.)

4 *Narrow* Why did Christ liken the Christian life to a narrow way? (Matthew 7.13–14; 21–23; Mark 10.23–27; John 6.60–71.)

Serious business

'The door to heaven is narrow. Work hard to get in . . .' (Luke 13.24 Living Bible).

ROUGH AND READY

The group were still very rough and ready. They had an incorrigible bent for bargaining ... and sacred and secular would sometimes get terribly mixed ...

'I'll buy your shirt.'

'But my shirt is not for sale, friend. I haven't come to trade with you ... Look again at this picture. This is why I've come ...'

What, No Tobacco? ... 5

5 What, No Tobacco?

'Didn't you bring any sugar?'

'No.'

'Chewing tobacco?'

'Sorry.'

'Well, what about smoking tobacco? Didn't you bring any of that?'

'Sorry, none of that either.'

'Well, don't come up here if you don't bring us what we like!'

This group of tribesfolk had a great facility for reducing you to size. If we hadn't known a little of their background —the times they had been taken down by strangers; the rugged life they lived, trying to carve a meagre living out of unwilling circumstances—we might have given up early.

But with all their seeming aggressiveness they were a most colourful and likeable people. I asked old father Inchi why he was so bound to the tobacco weed that he would almost sell his birthright for a *kati* of it.

'Ah, tobacco for us is like milk to a baby. We can't live without it', he replied.

He had a graveyard cough and spat profusely with every spasm. Both he and his people were simply riddled with TB. Not many of them arrived at a good old age. In giving them medicine I always reminded them that my fighting their coughs was a losing battle. The best medicine for them was to break with the weed. But how can a man break from something he's idolized from a child? I knew the answer, and told them often of Jesus' power to make us into new creatures.

After a while, several of this community did turn to the Lord, giving us reason to visit them more often, though at best this was only twice a year owing to their remote situation. They live on the edge of a cantankerous little river, winding and rapid-strewn, whose length we poled in our small canoe. We now travel in more style, powered by an outboard engine which revolutionizes the journey.

ROUGH AND READY

Though followers of the Christian way, the group were
still very rough and ready. They had an incorrigible bent
for bargaining and in the early days, sacred and secular
would sometimes get terribly mixed when their eye for a
deal would overcome them during worship.

'I'll buy your shirt.'

'But my shirt is not for sale, friend. I haven't come to
trade with you, as I said before. Look again at this picture.
This is why I've come.'

'But I'll give you a good jungle knife for it.'

I knew that he would have given me a jungle knife for
my shirt, but the last thing that I wanted in these parts
was to be called a trader.

These folk are the master jungle knife makers of the area.
People from miles around make the tortuous river journey
to see them, bringing their bars of mild steel for these
jungle blacksmiths to work on. And there the craftsmen sit
in their little, lean-to forges, cigarette in mouth, arm
muscles at the stretch as they pound the heated steel into
shape. At night, dogs sidle up to the warm ashes while
their masters go to work with their files, sharpening up the
blades that they have worked on through the day. Then,
with the finished article, comes the bargaining.

'I'll pay you two measures of rice', a trader would offer.

'Nonsense, I've worked on this knife for a whole day and
made a handle and sheath into the bargain. Have pity on
my tired flesh.'

But so often their tired flesh was not pitied. They were
poorly rewarded with a pittance of rice or a fistful of
tobacco.

Our meetings with them were often filled with surprises.
It was an achievement to get the Christians all together
in one place at one time. They were so unused to anything
organized.

'Hats off. Cigarettes out just for a moment, friends. We
are praying to God.'

What a hardship to stub the weed for a while. Hungry
dogs circled the gathering, sniffing hopefully. They had

gnawed the leather handle of my brief-case in their search for food. A woman with a pet pig sat tickling its tummy with her foot as we continued our devotions. Men grunted their interest as they looked at the picture of Jesus.

'Look at that gown', one nudged the other, referring to the robe that Jesus was wearing. 'I'd buy that!'

'Look at the whiskers on his face. But his nose is like a white man's. What's his race? His eyes and skin are brown like ours.'

The story of Jesus' love and power continued with vivid background noises. The muffled running commentary from the audience was sustained right through.

In earlier days their shaky sapling floors forbad gatherings of more than a dozen. Any cracking noise in the structure would send the flock scrambling for the notched pole that led down to the safety of mother earth. The folk showed no surprise when I fell through the floor. I fancy they were expecting it. Although the ground was only a few feet below it was a bit unsettling and rather a letdown. But in dealing with these people one's equilibrium was best left at home.

WARMING TO THE GOOD NEWS

Did you ask about their progress? This developed slowly and became apparent not in any ability to cope with the creed but rather in the little acts of kindness and understanding by which they let us know that we were getting through. They were not given to hospitality towards outsiders, and for someone like me to be offered a little of their boiled tapioca was indeed progress. Jesus said: 'He that receives you, receives me.' I often thought of that concerning these folk. It was a red-letter day when I was offered some of their precious jungle sago. They would cook it for me, they said.

The cooking of it was as interesting as the eating. First, a sleeping dog had to be evicted from the large cooking bowl. The bowl was then given a little swill with some water from a bamboo container. Then some more water was poured into it. As it heated, the sago was gently crumbled into it and the liquid stirred until it became a thick, glutinous mass. My portion was served up on a tin plate and eaten with relish. Then the dog got his bowl back with the reward of something to lick. I felt that I was now one of the 'in' group.

One day I received a message from a village elder who was one of the Christian group. 'I want you to come over and make a name for my new granddaughter.' In fact, he wanted the baby prayed over and commended to the Lord as well. After some teaching to this little family circle, I asked the old man what kind of name he had in mind for the baby. 'I want a name from the Book', he replied. From the list of names that I mentioned, 'Lydia' was eventually chosen, although I could see that they were in for trouble with the pronunciation. But Lydia was what they wanted. So we prayed over Lydia, commending her and her family to God. When I visited the group some months later I asked after the health of Lydia but got no response.

'Lydia? Who's Lydia?' Nobody had heard of Lydia.

'Oh, you mean India! Little India; she's fine.'

The community of Christians has grown over the years as family after family has parted with the spirit world of the Bungan cult and thrown in their lot with Christ. Eleven of their children have begun attending a local school, a great advance for a folk whose suspicions that school would put ideas into the kids' heads had long held back their progress. A few have been baptized and were growing in the Lord when last I saw them.

Rough diamonds, it is true. But I think their faith has the smell of the forge and the forest upon it, a kind of simplicity that God loves.

Guidelines

Foolish

'Few of you were wise, or powerful, or of high social status, from the human point of view. God purposely chose what the world considers nonsense...' (1 Corinthians 1.26–27 TEV).

Wise

'But God has brought you into union with Christ Jesus, and God has made Christ to be our wisdom; by him we are put right with God, we become God's own people, and are set free' (1 Corinthians 1.30 TEV).

Talkback

1 *Uncouth?* 'Better uncouth life than aesthetic death', says a writer. What has the Bible to say along these lines? (Isaiah 35.8; Matthew 23.27–28; 1 Corinthians 1.21–31.)

2 *Break* What Bible teaching would you give in endeavouring to help these folk overcome their lifelong addiction to tobacco? (Leviticus 11.44–45; Ezekiel 36.24–27; 1 Corinthians 6.19–20; 2 Corinthians 5.17–18.)

3 *Hygiene* Would you think for hygiene's sake a missionary should take his own food on trips? (1 Corinthians 9.19–23; Hebrews 2.14–18.)

4 *Nice shirt!* A man in this story wanted to buy my shirt. Should I have *given* it to him? (Matthew 5.42; Luke 12.13–15; James 1.5.)

Where can I get wisdom?

'If ... any of you does not know how to meet any particular problem he has only to ask God ... But he must ask in sincere faith without secret doubts as to whether he really wants God's help or not' (James 1.5–6, J. B. Phillips).

THE DEATH-DRUMMER

We wanted so much to pray...indeed to do anything to put a spoke in the works of this eerie progression. Finally, my colleague held the drummer's hands as we shouted for quiet through the hysteria.

'Please, hold the noise... Don't let the bad spirit deceive you any longer... Let us ask Jesus to give us peace ...'

Death-drummer's Beat ... 6

6 Death-drummer's Beat

As our boat pulled in to the edge of the river, men, women and children, on the banks for their evening bathe, quickly gravitated to the scene of our arrival.

'Where have you come from?' they asked with the typical boldness of their clan.

'And why have you been so long in coming?'

'And who's this?' asked one, pointing his chin in my direction. My colleague made the introduction.

'A new missionary, eh? He looks scared.'

How right they were. As I looked up towards the tall, dark and forbidding longhouses that lay beneath the damp shade of some towering hardwoods, I felt weak at the knees. Was I going to have to live in there? And with these aggressive folk? I felt as though I was being taken to prison.

I'd told the folk back home that none of these things was going to move me; that my God was real and that He would be strong to help. And now, here at my first real encounter with the people I'd been sent to, things seemed so different from what I'd expected. I felt that the Lord was going to have to do some big things in connection with my survival. How vivid were those first impressions! How potent the prayers of folk back home!

We had spent a wearying day travelling upstream. At times our plucky little engine could only give the barest forward propulsion to our 54-foot longboat as we battled against the violent eddies and lashing rapids of this wild river. On several occasions our crew had taken to a lilting war cry as they battled with the spray-tossed stream, plunging in their paddles to give that little extra jerking movement that sent our boat hesitantly through the worst of the currents.

The primaeval forests that lined the river banks, growth upon growth, trees, ferns and vines, offered us no help apart from their shade and the promise that there may be a stray creeper to cling to should we come to grief in the turmoil. We were glad to arrive at the tribal village at sundown.

On entering the first house, we had hardly sat down when the headman burst in unannounced. He was a tall fellow, rather old but erect as a bean-pole. He came decked in a black loincloth which he quickly brushed aside, baring the back of his thigh and a fiery, red boil.

'Give me something for this', he barked, without any introduction.

'Is that the way you shake hands with your visitors?' an onlooker teased him. The chief smiled and pressed his case. We opened the medicine kit and found something for him.

UPROAR

It was next day that the pandemonium broke loose. The normal jingle of crowing cocks, skirmishing dogs and bustling people was suddenly inundated by terrified shouts and wails and the frenzied beating of a drum. Someone had died. The death was not unexpected, for it was that of an old village elder who had been waning for some time.

As we walked along the river's edge and scaled the notched pole up to the pathetic scene, I was petrified. There were some weird goings on.

The old man's body, wrinkled with history, had been brought out from the smoky room on to the longhouse verandah. A couple of distraught women sat stroking the body while, above the general din of weeping, another woman sat howling out a tearful lamentation. She hoped that the dead man would have a safe journey to the mysterious land of the shadows.

Little children wandered freely around the corpse, some stroking it and imitating the grief of their parents. Dogs sniffed around the throng, fighting for a right-of-way between the mourners. But the spine-tingling thing to me was an old tribesman's frantic hammering of that deer-hide drum that had been strung with rattan cords from a lower beam.

It was my first close-up experience of a tribal death.

Although there were some signs of Christian faith in this village, things were still very rough and ready. It often takes years of systematic teaching to wipe out the crude and sinister impressions that have come through even to the young from the centuries of pagan practice and prejudice. These people had been followers of the Christian Way for only a short while. They were largely illiterate, very untaught, but full of spirit.

I watched the drummer's face. He was shaking with emotion. Being only a stone's throw away from a pagan mentality, the folk were still oppressed with the notion that the dead man's spirit might at any moment swoop to take one of the living with him to the kingdom of the dead. The drummer was doing all in his power to ward off the potential intruder.

We wanted so much to pray, to tell them of Jesus' power, indeed to do anything Christian to put a spoke in the works of this eerie progression. Was the devil to have an unimpeded run and stampede the people back into his fold? We spoke to the drummer asking him to stop his noise. It seemed that he was responsible for whipping up much of the fever. He gave us the merest grunt, being too hypnotized by his art. The fate of his people was at stake, or that's how he felt. Finally, my colleague held his hands as we shouted for quiet through the hysteria.

'Please, hold the noise, friends; all of you. Don't let the bad spirit deceive you any longer. Jesus has defeated him. Let us ask Jesus to give us peace.'

Quietness came slowly as the people began to break step with the devil and call haltingly upon the name of Jesus.

AN OLD CUSTOM PREVAILS

In front of the body the coffin now lay prepared. By this time the corpse had been wrapped in a clean sarong and crowned with a dome-shaped, raffia hat. After the short break for prayer, a woman's hysteria brought back the shindy to an awful crescendo as the body was lifted by four men into the coffin. This was also the drummer's invitation to return to his carnival. If the dead man's spirit was going to victimize, now was the critical time just as the body was being lowered into its encasement. The drummer worked like a man possessed.

Then, a strange thing happened. Before the coffin was sealed, a man pushed into the inner circle carrying a jungle knife, a bundle of rice and a change of clothes. These were meticulously placed alongside the body in the coffin.

'But wait a minute, friends. What's the meaning of these?' my colleague questioned.

'He may need them for the journey', the relatives replied. They explained a little sheepishly that the dead man would need the food for such a long and perilous excursion into the mysterious other world. And what if he should meet with enemies? Impossible to think of him travelling without his jungle knife!

It was not easy to present Christian teaching in such a highly-charged situation, but the knife and other things were reluctantly removed from the coffin at our request. However, the folk were not convinced that the dead man was safe without these provisions for his journey. They were disturbed for his welfare and feared that his spirit would come to grief. A little deception had to take place to remedy the situation, they felt. Before the coffin was taken over the river to its final resting place it was hurried around to the back of the longhouse where swift helpers quickly whipped off the lid and again slipped in the knife, the rice and the change of clothes. It was years later that they told us about this.

Now, they find comfort in the thrilling words of the Lord Jesus which they can read in their own language : 'I am the resurrection and the life. Whoever believes in me will live, even though he dies ... There are many rooms in my Father's house, and I am going to prepare a place for you' (John 11.25; 14.2 TEV).

Guidelines

United to whom?
'For just as all men die because of their union to Adam, in the same way all will be raised to life because of their union to Christ' (I Corinthians 15.22 TEV).

Talkback

1 *Fear* Why do you think pagan people are so terrified of death? (Romans 5.12; Romans 6.23; Hebrews 9.27.)
2 *Hope* If you were the missionary at this funeral service, what would you teach the people? (John 5.24; John 11.25–26; Hebrews 2.14–15.)
3 *Preach or teach?* Do you think teaching new converts is as important as planting new churches? (Matthew 28.18–20; Acts 20.17–21; Ephesians 4.11–15.)
4 *Frightener* If a man fired his gun every few minutes on the way to the graveyard to ward off evil spirits, what teaching would you give? (Mark 1.27; 5.36; 1 Corinthians 15.55–57; 1 John 5.4–5.)

Listen

'. . . I am telling you this strange and wonderful secret : we shall not all die, but we shall all be given new bodies! It will all happen in a moment, in the twinkling of an eye, when the last trumpet is blown. For there will be a trumpet blast from the sky and all the Christians who have died will suddenly become alive with new bodies that will never, never die; and then we who are still alive shall suddenly have new bodies too' (1 Corinthians 15.51–52 Living Bible).

SHOCK TREATMENT

'Katim, is this a medicine man that you have here?'

'Well, er...' Katim's embarrassment gave the game away.

'Look, Katim, I can't pray for you until this man has gathered up his things and left this house.'

On hearing this, the medicine man stood up quickly and swung around on the missionary. 'I'm ministering to Katim in the name of the prophet Samuel', he said...

Playing with Fire ... 7

7　Playing with Fire

The little township was busy. The Chinese traders were overjoyed at the briskness of business, arising from the influx of tribespeople who had come to sell their rice and jungle produce. It was the after-harvest break when most enterprising tribesmen snatch at the opportunity of a trip to the bright lights and gaudy attractions of the towns.

Kimbalo, the ex-witchdoctor, was there too. He was a popular character and nodded greetings to his many acquaintances as he walked the streets in his gay clothes. He loved bright colours. Not everybody knew that he was supposed to be a Christian now and had presumably given over the shady practices which made him a man to be feared in days past.

But suddenly Kimbalo stood still and stared at the doleful approach of a young friend, who seemed in deep distress.

'What is it? Why do you look so sad, Along?' Kimbalo asked.

'Someone has stolen my money', Along replied.

Kimbalo thought for a moment and his brow furrowed. He coughed hesitantly and turned again to Along.

'Along, how can this be? How did it happen?'

The lad related the story of the loss that had occurred at the town lodging house. He told of how he had been doing casual work to get a few dollars for some presents to take home to his village. And now his money had gone.

'Along, would you like me to help you?' Kimbalo offered.

'Yes, but how can you help?'

'Come over into this coffee shop, my son, and you will see.'

KIMBALO'S OLD ART

Kimbalo offered Along a seat in a secluded corner of the coffee shop and went over to order two coffees from the Chinese shopkeeper. When the drinks arrived, Kimbalo placed one of the cups before him and began nervously to recall an old art.

'My son, do you really want me to help you?' Kimbalo seemed hesitant.

'Yes, uncle, it was all the money I had, every bit.'

Kimbalo sat for a moment staring into the coffee. Then, after a few mystical exercises over the cup he turned to Along again. 'Now, my son, tell me, do you recognize the face you now see marked out in the froth of this coffee?'

Along seemed a little startled.

'Yes, uncle, this is the face of the fellow who sleeps beside me at our lodging place.'

'He is the thief!' Kimbalo's voice rose with indignation. 'Go to him and get your money back.'

Along was astounded at the revelation, but went shyly to do as his mentor had said. He returned later to tell Kimbalo that his prediction was right. The money had been recovered.

'Kimbalo, why do you do this kind of thing?' a Christian friend asked, after hearing of the episode with Along. 'Don't you realize that it is wrong for Christians to meddle in things like this?'

'I know', Kimbalo replied, never lost for an answer. 'But you see, things are different now. Before, I used to do it for the devil. Now I do it for the Lord.'

Kimbalo died soon after, a man of doubtful standing in his church. It seemed that the devil had him on a long lead.

THE DOUBTFUL HELPER

'Will you please come and pray for Katim. He's sick', said the caller.

'Does he want medicine too or just prayer?' the missionary queried.

'He's been sick so long. Come and see.'

The missionary was taken to the little home of Katim, who had been ill with some strange affliction for many weeks.

'Can we come up?' the escort enquired as they arrived

at the foot of Katim's steps. There seemed to be something of a mild scramble inside followed by a weak voice inviting the visitors to enter. But as the missionary went through the door of the sick man's room, he noticed an unfamiliar figure sitting over in one corner, with averted face. He sensed that something was wrong as he walked over to the other corner where the sick man lay. Katim strained up on one arm to greet his guests. The missionary felt that he'd better come straight to the point of a worrying thought that had occurred to him as he entered.

'Katim, is this a medicine man that you have here?'

'Well, er . . .' Katim's embarrassment gave the game away.

'Look, Katim, I can't pray for you until this man has gathered up his things and left this house.'

On hearing this, the medicine man stood up quickly and swung around on the missionary. 'I'm ministering to Katim in the name of the prophet Samuel', he said.

'Well, that may be so. But I'm not praying while you are here. Will you please go, and take all your medicines and paraphernalia with you', the missionary answered.

Katim did not improve. His condition seemed to go from bad to worse, until his people decided to bring him around to the mission house as a last resort. But he did no better there, and after a few days went berserk and fled into the jungle. Folk said that Katim's life was beclouded by the medicine man's art, right to the end.

Do you wonder what God thinks of the practices of magic and mysticism? Then listen to these words of His to His people the Jews : 'There shall not be found among you any one . . . who practices divination, a soothsayer, or an augur, or a sorcerer, or a charmer, or a medium, or a wizard, or a necromancer. For whoever does these things is an abomination to the Lord.' (Deuteronomy 18.10–12a RSV).

Guidelines

If you forsake the Lord ...
'You cannot serve the Lord; for he is a holy God; he is a jealous God; he will not forgive your transgressions or your sins. If you forsake the Lord and serve foreign gods, then he will turn and do you harm, and consume you, after having done you good.' (Joshua 24.19–20 RSV).

Talkback

1 *Suspect* On what grounds would you suspect Kimbalo's profession to be a Christian? (Deuteronomy 18.10–12; Matthew 7.16–20; 2 Timothy 2.19.)

2 *Excuse* Thinking about Kimbalo's excuse for his art that the end justifies the means, what Scriptures warn us against the dangers of this dictum? (Genesis 3.1–7; Luke 4.1–4.)

3 *Warning* Can you think of any Scriptures that warn us about the practices of phoney practitioners working in the Lord's name? (Deuteronomy 13.1–5; Isaiah 56.10–11; Jeremiah 6.13–14; Matthew 7.15, 21–23; Mark 13.22.)

4 *Credibility* What Scriptures help us in determining the credibility of Christians whose lives don't line up with what they profess? (1 John 4.1–3; 1 Corinthians 12.3; 13.1–3; Galatians 1.6–9; 6.14.)

Test them

'My dear friends : do not believe all who claim to have the Spirit, but test them to find out if the spirit they have comes from God' (1 John 4.1 TEV).

THE FORTUNE TELLER'S PREDICTION

The fortune teller stroked his chin and Tassi noticed his brow beginning to furrow.

'Your hand does not bring us good news...' he said. 'Your wife is going to die in childbirth...'

The tribesman's mouth dropped. Drawing his hand back, he... began moving out of the room.

'Hey!' yelled the fortune teller. 'That will be five dollars.'

Witchdoctor's Reverse ... 8

8 Witchdoctor's Reverse

'Well, where's the rice?' asked Maria. Her husband, Tassi, had just shuffled into the room on returning from the local bazaar, a 20 minute canoe-journey away.

'What rice?' he questioned.

'Well, didn't you sell the fish you caught so that you could buy some rice? What happened?' Tassi hung his head. Two hours before, he had left for the bazaar with a fine ten-pound fish which he had hooked that morning. The feel of it on his line, ah, there was nothing like it. And as their year's rice supply had now come to an end, Tassi concluded that the spirits had been good to him for once, in providing an alternate means of getting a small amount of the staple food.

Folk quickly gathered around him as he walked up the steps of the bazaar verandah. There were always many keen buyers for fish and Tassi prepared himself for the siege. First he popped through a door to borrow a shop-keeper's scales and then, placing them beside him, unsheathed his jungle knife and began cutting up his catch.

The dollars and cents rolled in quickly and before long he had a small bundle of them forming a healthy mound in his right-hand trouser pocket. This was normally quite barren except for his small tobacco roll.

The head was the last part of the fish to go. And now, Tassi's mind began to turn towards ways of spending his newly acquired 5 dollars and 50 cents. Yes, he supposed he could buy the rice. He could buy anything, come to that. In fact he felt rather rich and frivolous. After all, people don't come by easy money like this every day. What about having a little flutter, a little peep into the future?

Right nearby was a Chinese fortune teller. Clutching the wad of notes in his pocket, he appealed to the soothsayer in his best out-of-luck voice. Fate hadn't been kind to him, he said. Tassi looked at the fortune teller as if a little palmistry could consign all his fears and premonitions into oblivion.

THE OMINOUS PREDICTION

'Let's have a look at your hand', said the fortune teller. Tassi laid it out straight, palm upwards, on the table.

'Mmmmm', the fortune teller stroked his chin and Tassi noticed his brow beginning to furrow. 'Your hand does not bring us good news. You have had a bad spin, you say? I'm afraid things are not going to improve.'

Tassi prepared for the worst.

'Your wife is soon going to die in childbirth.'

The tribesman's mouth dropped. Drawing his hand back, he pushed his chair aside, and, head down, began moving out of the room.

'Hey!' yelled the fortune teller. 'That will be five dollars.'

Tassi paid him and walked giddily out on to the bazaar footway. His wife was already eight months pregnant. How on earth would he be able to break the news to her. Feeling his way along to the last shop he wandered in and bought 50 cents worth of biscuits, as if these would be able to substitute for the unbought rice. At least they might take some of the pain out of the message he had to bring to his waiting spouse.

Tassi now faced her. 'Well, Maria, I did hope to get some rice for the fish, but on second thoughts I concluded it would be best if we could know what the spirits had in store for us. So I called in to see Hock Liang, the fortune teller . . .'

He cleared his throat and turned around to face her.

'Maria, listen to me. Hock Liang has some bad news for us. He says that you are going to die in this childbirth.'

The news broke Maria. She sobbed her heart out until Tassi said he would go to the witchdoctor for a second opinion. The Chinese fortune teller could have been mistaken, surely. Maria had been feeling quite well up till this time and had not had a lot of trouble in previous births.

The witchdoctor gazed at her and after performing his ritual came down with his assessment. The spirits had decreed that Maria was going to die, and die she would. The whole thing seemed outrageous to Tassi. What had he done to provoke the wrath of the spirits like this? Maria was crushed with fear. No one was able to comfort her. Anyway, what could anyone say? The spirits had spoken and her life was soon to be snuffed out like that of a stray dog.

'*Nasib*', everyone said. 'It's just her luck.'

A FRIEND IN NEED

But down at the government dispensary was a friend, Julia, the midwife. She had never let them down and perhaps this time she would at least lend a listening ear to their tragic story. She was a Christian, too, and these Christians always seemed to be able to give some sort of an answer about religious things. Everyone liked Julia; she made people feel comfortable.

After giving Maria an examination, Julia tried to comfort them, popping a ten-dollar bill into Tassi's hand as they left. With this Tassi bought two measures of much-needed rice and used the rest to pay the witchdoctor. Must keep on the right side of him. He had his own sinister way of dealing with outstanding debts.

The fateful night soon arrived. 'Julia, Julia, wake up! It's me, Tassi.'

'Who's that?'

'It's me! Maria is in labour. Come quickly. You must help.'

Julia stirred from her bed with unusual sluggishness. Each foot felt like lead. Her head spun. No, she couldn't face it. Wasn't Maria's fate sealed anyway? Why interfere? Let the people get sick of this kind of thing and perhaps they'll come to their senses. But it was no use. Julia just had to go.

'All right, wait there, I'm coming.' Julia prayed as she walked along, tagging behind Tassi.

BATTLE FOR A LIFE

The room was dark except for the little fire and a flickering lamp beside Maria. A couple of tribal matrons hovered over her, trying to encourage her in her half-hearted battle with fate.

'All of you be quiet now! We are starting afresh', declared Julia, taking a position of command. 'I'm going to pray.' The matrons gathered up their chattels and moved aside.

'O Lord, I'm just not clever', Julia prayed aloud. 'Every bit of cleverness for this job must come from you. Lord, please look at Maria and have mercy upon her.'

'Things are going to be quite all right, Maria', Julia said, more in hope than anything. 'You must trust our God.'

Within a couple of hours Maria gave birth to a baby boy and by morning the crisis had passed. She was going to be all right and so was the child.

'Well', said the witchdoctor as he heard the news of the safe arrival of Maria's son. 'Well, anyway, let's think about a good spirit-powered name for him.'

'Ah no, you don't have to bother now', replied Tassi. 'We're saying farewell to the spirits today. Our son is to have a Christian name. We are becoming Christians like Julia.'

Though her body felt like a wet rag, Julia was jubilant on arriving back home. Taking a pen, she opened the large, midwife's baby book that lay on her table and made an entry :

'Samuel, son of Tassi and Maria...' and she wrote the date.

Guidelines

The murderer
'...the devil...was a murderer from the beginning...' (John 8.44 RSV).

The Lifegiver
'Jesus said... I am the way, and the truth, and the life...' (John 14.6 RSV).

Talkback

1 *Fortune* Do you think it right to go to a fortune teller or consult the stars just for fun? (Leviticus 19.31; 2 Corinthians 6.14–18; Ephesians 5.11–16.)

2 *Future* If Tassi asked you whether Christians had any way of finding out about the future, what would you tell him? (Psalm 37.3–5; Matthew 6.31–34; John 14.1–6; Philippians 1.21–23.)

3 *Heaven* If you were describing heaven to Tassi, what heavenly benefits do you think would really appeal to a man of his background? (John 14.2; Hebrews 11.10; Revelation 7.16–17; 21.4.)

4 *'Fate is the hunter'* 'Subjection to an immutable fate is an iron fetter that binds pagan minds'. What is the Christian answer to the fate mentality? (Genesis 1.1ff; Acts 17.23–31; Matthew 6.9–13; John 14.1–7; 27–28; John 15.15–16.)

Not fate, but FATHER!

'When you pray, say :
                    Father ...' (Luke 11.2 RSV).

LONGING EYES

Balan and his family had been watching with longing eyes the progress of the little band of Christians ... Some had been healed ... in the name of this one, Jesus, whom the Christians worshipped. And Julia the midwife? If that's what Christians were all about, Balan and his family wanted to be Christians ... They'd make the change at this time without delay ...

The Fine that Backfired ... 9

9 The Fine that Backfired

'These Christians are getting stronger!'

'And more brazen!'

'They'll be taking over the longhouse next!'

A cluster of the village wise men was in conference. What would their goddess, Bungan, think about this Christian group springing up right under their noses? They decided that they would have to do something to stem the tide or in some way try and make it up to their deity lest she get cold feet.

The most recent thing that had got under their skins was the birth of the baby, Samuel Tassi, which had brought another family into the Christian fold.

As it was harvest-festival-time for the pagans, the witch-doctors decided that they would pile on the devotions and make a grandiose token offering. 'Let's call our friends and neighbours from far and wide and let them drink with us; let them eat their fill and see something of the splendour of our regard for our goddess—Bungan, the wife of God.'[1]

In keeping with this scheme, certain men were sent off to the forest to cut some stout poles and bring them back to the longhouse. Then they erected a large wooden stand that looked something like a cross on the longhouse verandah.

When all was ready the witchdoctors sent a call throughout the village, 'Tell the people to come and pay homage to Bungan. Let everyone bring the best of their riches and bedeck the stand. Come, honour Bungan, the giver of life

[1] Bungan—the wife of God

The cult called Bungan began in the late forties with a dream given to a tribesman in East Kalimantan (Indonesian Borneo). It soon spread to Sarawak among the Kenyah and Kayan tribes. Its deity is 'Bungan—the wife of God'.

This is a modified form of animism in which the ceremonial offering of chicken and eggs play a large part. It is now dying out with its old and largely illiterate leaders. The younger, educated generation consider it a religion of the backwoods because it is bookless and reeks of an age they have left behind. The Gospel has taken many converts from Bungan.

and wealth, the provider of our *padi*, the sustainer of our children.'

The folk turned out with the best of their possessions : fine *batik* sarongs, jungle knives, precious beads, brass gongs. The stand was soon embellished with a riot of pagan wealth. Every pagan family had made an offering. It was now up to Bungan to respect their worship and do them good. The visitors would be coming in a day or so.

FLY IN THE OINTMENT

Everything seemed to be going nicely until the following morning when someone noticed that a gaping hole had developed in the chain of offerings surrounding the stand. Someone had removed an offering. What an insult to Bungan! What a blatant provocation to throw in the teeth of their deity, and at such a sensitive time as this. The witchdoctors were indignant and the village shaken.

Who had done this thing? He would have to be suitably punished and the wrath of Bungan appeased. A search was made for the culprit. He was not hard to find.

'Yes, I removed our offering', said Balan. The folk had tracked the offence down to him.

'I removed it because I've changed my mind.'

Balan and his family had been watching with longing eyes the progress of the little band of Christians among them. They had noticed how some of them had been healed of their ills in the name of this one, Jesus, whom the Christians worshipped. And Julia, the midwife? If that's what Christians were all about, Balan and his family wanted to be Christians. They decided that they'd make the change at this time without further delay.

The witchdoctors were thrown into confusion.

'By hook or by crook Balan will have to pay for this insult. A shadow has been cast over our village', they declared.

In due course they relayed to Pejau, the village headman, their advice regarding the fine; something to make Balan smart and be a warning to others. Balan was fined a brass gong, a jungle knife and some money.

'It's not me that's fining you', said the headman apologetically. He was a gracious soul. 'This fine falls on you from our custom. I know it is heavy, but we must honour Bungan.'

Balan listened to the sentence with a heavy heart. He had nothing against the headman, for he knew him to be a kindly old fellow who had always tried to govern the village with due regard to all the cross currents of opinion.

But Balan was poor. And he certainly did not feel like recanting from his act, to restore his offering to Bungan. But neither did he relish the idea of going into debt to pay the fine.

The whole thing provided a juicy point for village gossip. The fining of Balan made the Bungan devotees feel pure and exalted.

But the Christians were incensed. 'Nonsense', they said. 'This is beyond the pale. Why should a man have to pay to change his custom?' They confronted the pagan leaders with their opinions in very predictable terms, until Pastor Elia, the local Christian leader, called to encourage them to take a wiser stand. He agreed that Balan had been wronged. 'But let's tell God all about it and let Him work it out for us', he said.

PATIENCE REWARDED

Julia, the Christian midwife, took a similar stand as Balan stood before her pouring out his tale of woe.

'Nothing good will come of a lot of squabbling, Balan. I know you've got no money. But what if I pay the fine for you, to put an end to any ill-feeling between us and the pagans.'

Julia paid the fine, in providing the prescribed brass gong, the jungle knife and money, giving them to the village leaders on Balan's behalf. Balan was sobered and grateful. It was things like this about the Christians that had humbled him all along.

The leaders received the fine with equanimity and again rehearsed the implications of it all. Yes, the fine was heavy. But it had to be. They consoled one another.

But something wasn't right somewhere; there was a cat among the chickens. Rumours began to buzz along the long-house verandah as folk chewed over a very curly piece of confusion. Balan had been given the fine but Julia had paid it. And Julia was the headman's very own daughter! The witchdoctors were called into emergency session, and after long deliberation they came to a humbling decision.

'This is a tricky situation', they confessed. 'Village opinion is mounting against this fine because it has now fallen upon Julia, a most respected one. She must be spared the indignity. The implements of the fine must be returned to her and the case dismissed.' They would ask the head-man himself to convey to his daughter the apologies of all concerned.

'I trust you will understand all that's happened', said Pejau, as he faced his daughter to return the implements of the fine.

'Here is the gong and the jungle knife, Julia. And here is the money, less ten dollars for the witchdoctors' expenses.'

Balan, Julia and all the Christians rejoiced together at God's overruling in this most unexpected way. What next would He do to help them?

Guidelines

Helping hand
'Two are better than one ... For if they fall, one will lift up his fellow' (Ecclesiastes 4.9-10 RSV).

Honoured
God says: '... those who honour me I will honour' (1 Samuel 2.30 RSV).

Talkback

1   *Response*   Balan was a poor person. Do you think that

the poor and oppressed are more likely to respond to the good news than the well-fed and economically secure? Should we aim at any particular social stream in our preaching? (1 Samuel 2.7–8; Matthew 5.3; 11.4–5; 27.57; 1 Corinthians 12.13; Hebrews 13.5–6.)

2 *Fined* How would you have advised Balan about yielding to pagan authorities in this matter of conscience : to pay the fine or protest? (Romans 13.1–3; Matthew 22.20–21; Acts 5.27–29.)

3 *Reaction* What should be the typical reaction of a Christian to suffering for his faith? (2 Timothy 3.12; Matthew 5.11–12; 1 Peter 2.18–25.)

4 *In debt* Most pagans feel hopelessly in debt to the spirit world. How then is the Gospel such wonderful news? (Isaiah 61.1; John 8.31–32; Romans 8.2, 21; Colossians 2.15.)

Look up!

'Keep your eyes on Jesus, our leader and instructor. He was willing to die a shameful death on the cross because of the joy he knew would be his afterwards; and now he sits in the place of honour by the throne of God' (Hebrews 12.2 Living Bible).

HEADMAN'S DILEMMA

The headman coughed, pulled in his girth and boomed,
'Quiet!'

'Our village is now falling apart', he bellowed.

'Why are our young school-leavers moping around the
longhouse staring at books when they should be out with a
jungle knife? Why are our fruit gardens getting all overgrown? Why are our young men always racing off with
something to trade...?'

Who's Coming to Town?...10

'Gau, come here.'

Gau put down his basket of bamboo water-containers and scrambled up the stairs that led to the headman's verandah.

'Listen, Gau. Go and tell the missionary I want to see him. And be quick about it.'

The headman was sitting in his familiar cane chair when I arrived. He was a big man with a large head and an enormous laugh. He loved to hear his own voice and believed that there is 'beauty in the bellow of a blast.' Yet he was a jovial character and most likeable.

He had recently been disturbed about the enormous abdomen he was developing and asked my advice as to how he could lose weight.

'How many leaf packs of rice do you eat at each meal?' I asked.

'Oh, about four to six!' he replied with a boyish grin.

'Well, what about cutting it down to two? And do you think you could cope with a jog around the village each day?'

He laughed at the jog idea. But he promised to try the diet.

Then he said, 'Look, we've got problems in our village. I want you and your friends to come along tonight to a village conference.'

'What will we discuss?' I asked.

'Ah, it's difficult, Lalong', he replied, addressing me by my Bornean name. 'Too many of our people are deserting the village for the towns. Our old people are being neglected, our fruit gardens and rubber plots are untouched and our rice farms are being poorly made. People are getting obsessed with the towns.'

He spat and spun round on his chair to look down on the river. A cluster of youths had been loading a boat with some cane baskets of pigs and fowls in preparation for a trip to the coast. I had seen some of these local lads and

lassies with their little pop group of guitars, chinking
bottles and tin-lid cymbals in action in the Sunday morning
service.

Several of them had spent three years at a high school on
the coast. All had tasted something of the fruits of a little
education : the ability to read and write, to trade and to
get work in the town. The comforts and security of town
life had become attractive to them.

'But we'll talk about all this tonight. What about you
folk eating at my place first?' he offered. He was a wonderful host, kind and open-hearted.

The village 'palava'

The headman's verandah was crowded with men for the
night meeting. The women were not invited. They were at
home with the children. One or two of the fathers dandled
children on their knees, grounds for making an early
retreat should the proceedings get boring.

The headman coughed, pulled in his girth and boomed,
'Quiet!'

Following a long verbal itinerary through the village's
history, he got to the point of the night's 'palava.'

'Our village is now falling apart', he bellowed, 'It's true
the price of rubber has declined, and the rice price isn't
what it was. But we've faced these things before and come
through. Why are our young school-leavers moping around
the longhouse staring at books when they should be out
with a jungle knife in their hands? Why are our fruit
gardens getting all overgrown? Why are our young men
always racing off with something to trade? Look at them
again this morning.'

No one answered. Who dared?

'I'll tell you why. They've forgotten these uplands that
succoured them from babes. Their hearts are turning to
stone regarding their old folk that fought to get them this
land and sweated to make it workable. Instead, they're
going raving mad for the towns, the radios, the picture
theatres, the women, the money! Bah!'

As he was talking I was thinking a few things through.

A lot of educated young folk were getting impatient with life in the mountains. They said that the jungle knife gave them blisters. I knew, too, that they'd smarted at times on their coastal excursions at being referred to as 'hill-folk', people of the jungle, backwoodsmen! Farm life had been given a stigma.

THE PULL OF TOWN LIFE

Now the seeming ease of life in the towns—its readiness with food, medical facilities and the possibilities for material advancement—spoke progress to them.

The alternative, they thought, was to vegetate in the interior, on the edge of this wild river, hemmed in by rugged and infertile mountain country. If they did manage to grow anything in these parts with a view to trade, transporting it to market on this turbulent stream would soon gobble up all the profits. Education had put thoughts into their heads of making a better life for themselves, their wives and children. I was thinking of all this when the headman nodded in my direction.

'What are we going to do? What does the missionary say about all this? His people have faced all this kind of thing. Come, missionary, you teach us.'

We hadn't had rain for several days and the stickiness of the night didn't make for comfort. As I stood up to speak I could see the room was well sprinkled with the young folk the headman was slating. Some of them had newly finished school. A mug of coffee near my chair toppled over as I felt for footroom.

'Go! Get out of here!' yelled an elder, talking to a dog that was slinking across the floor with a stolen biscuit in its mouth.

'Quiet, let him speak', the headman came in, looking again at me. I'd been glad of the extra moment's grace to offer another prayer for help.

OTHER PEOPLE, SAME PROBLEM

'Fathers, brothers and sons, I'm not clever at this kind of thing, but my heart is with you and the Lord is for you.

Let us pray to start with. Our Big Father has answers to all things like this.' The air became easier as we unloaded the burden. The Bible says, 'casting all your care upon him.' We felt so much better after we'd talked to the Lord.

'This kind of thing that you face is not only your problem', I continued. 'It is occurring all over the world. The clever people tell us that within 30 years most people will be living in or near the towns.' I tried to make clear things which to the old must have seemed events of another planet; cruel and impersonal. They wanted to grow old and die where their hearts were—right here beneath the tall timbers.

'Ungrateful brats!' they said as they thought of the young. But they'd have little cause to fear. It was just the thought of being abandoned that made them gripe. Deep down they knew that their children would not leave them uncared for.

About two days' journey further inland was another village facing the same problem. I had noticed that a number of regulars at the church just weren't there any longer.

'They're down the coast on the palm oil scheme. Didn't you know?' I was sorry that I didn't know. It amounted to 12 per cent of the village roll-call. And others were preparing to go.

'But', I queried, 'They've been gone for months. For over a year some of them. Do you think they'll come back?'

'Maybe they will, maybe not.'

As this totalled about 80 souls from one little community, I wondered how many more there were experiencing a similar depletion. I had seen folk from the villages become hypnotized by the bright lights of the towns, weakened in their faith and rather destitute. They'd become street people in the towns.

Now, it was my colleague's turn to speak. How well he knew them! He was a veteran who had first preached to them some years before.

He stood up, beamed and reminded them of the day

they turned to the Lord. He also drew a smile as he reminded them of an incident prior to their turning to the Lord, in which they refused him and his wife entrance to their village, forcing the two of them to take refuge for the night under a *padi* storehouse.

Now, some of them were wanting to uproot and move. This was a time for good sense, he said, and for looking to their Father for guidance. He then informed them of a government resettlement scheme that might be of use to them should they decide later to move.

The chief then stopped fanning his tummy with his shirt, coughed commandingly and began gathering up the threads of the evening's proceedings.

They had plenty of fuel for their crack-of-dawn prayer meeting next day. And as we listened to them praying we knew that there could not be disunity in their village while they could pray together about their family problem.

Guidelines

Trust amid change
'Show me the path where I should go, O Lord; point out the right road for me to walk' (Psalm 25.4 Living Bible).

Talkback

1 *Involved* To what extent do you think missionaries should get involved in community problems? (Matthew 11.19; 14.14; John 6.5ff.)

2 *Generation gap* How would you try to bring a better understanding between the leisurely old and the impatient young in this village? (1 Peter 1.22; 5.5; 1 John 4.7–12.)

3 *Itchy feet* What Scriptural guidance would you have given these tribal youths with an itch for more of an urban life? (Genesis 13.11–13; Deuteronomy 11.29, 32; 1 John 2.15–17.)

4 *Aged* Do Christians have a direct responsibility for the

wellbeing of their old folk? What teaching would you give
on this? (Leviticus 19.32; Deuteronomy 27.16; Matthew
15.4; John 19.25–27; Ephesians 6.1–3.)

Looking for a better land?

The wrong way
'And Lot lifted up his eyes, and saw that the Jordan valley
was well watered everywhere... So Lot *chose for
himself*...' (Genesis 13.10–11 RSV).

The right way
'Tell me what to do, O Lord, and make it plain because
I am surrounded by waiting enemies' (Psalm 27.11 Living
Bible).

MEDICINE MAN'S ART

'...*when I looked in the jar there was a thing inside it moving around and disturbing the water. I asked the man what it was. "That, my friend, is the spirit of the person who has given you this sickness. Beside the jar there is a long needle; take it if you wish. If you plunge it down into the water, you will kill the person who has put this evil sickness upon you...*"'

Strange Medicine . . . 11

'Hullo, Juman, are you looking for something?' I called, speaking first, which was most unusual with this man.

'Oh no, I'm just working here in the long grass. Why are you so brave as to travel on such a big river as this?' he queried.

I took the mild rebuke. True, the river was swollen but not unnavigable. That was when I first discerned that something was not quite the same about Juman. We strolled up to his house together.

He was an old friend with a wonderful sense of humour that often sprang to life when he saw me : 'Hullo, here comes a stranger from the jungle.' He knew that I was just the opposite, but it made one feel good and welcome. Awing, his wife, was the same. She was not a Christian when she married Juman, but her heart had blossomed out to all that her husband taught her about the Christian faith.

'Awing, the missionary has come,' he called. There was a scuffle in the room and then the noise of a chair scraping the floor. Then Awing appeared, looking tired and strained. Something was indeed wrong and my heart felt heavy.

Before long, however, Awing had some biscuits and coffee prepared, which was a welcome in its way. Opening the door to the verandah she came through, placed the tray on the table and retired; it is a fairly normal Eastern custom for the men to eat alone. Yet I was pleased to see that she did pull up a chair and sit near the door. At least she could catch something of the conversation.

Juman poured the coffee. 'You shouldn't have gone to this trouble', I remarked, looking for an opening.

'It's nothing at all', he countered, 'you come so rarely !'

The coffee was sweet and most welcome. Juman brushed away some flies from the biscuits and placed them before me, near the glass of coffee. 'Drink well, you must be thirsty travelling in this heat.'

Normally we would have been in fits of laughter by now,

for he had a large fund of humorous stories for visitors. He also had a wonderful gift of seeing the funny side of his own misfortunes. It's hard to wear down a man like that. But now he could hardly crack a smile.

He emptied his coffee glass quickly and put it down.

A TIME OF TROUBLE

'We've needed you. We have been in great trouble', he opened up. 'Awing and I have been very, very sick. Almost despaired of our lives. We looked in vain for someone to help us and to pray with us, but there has been no one.'

'What's been the trouble? Tell me all about it. Everything.'

He swallowed to clear a lump in his throat and gazed down at the floor with his hands clasped between his knees. 'Ah, it's been difficult, difficult beyond words. We have had a strange sickness. Twice we made the long, long journey to the hospital on the coast. They gave us all kinds of medicine but it had no strength. We just got worse, that's all there was to it.'

'What kind of sickness was it?' I wanted to help.

'It was all so strange. I can hardly describe it. At one stage Awing became so ill that she asked me to get my gun and end her life. I said we would go to the coast again in a last desperate search for help. It was all so expensive. All our money has gone.'

'And did the hospital help you this time?'

'No, that's how we came to go astray', Juman continued. 'When we were at wits'-end corner we met some friends who advised us to go to a pagan medicine man with strong powers and he would fix us up. And we went. We knew it was wrong, but we were desperate.'

'And what did the medicine man do?'

'I will tell you it all tonight.'

At this Juman bounded up. He was loath to continue his story in the presence of the visitors who were now approaching. I looked forward to the further talk.

SINISTER DEALINGS

Awing joined us for the evening. She had a New Testament in her hand though her ability to read it was limited.

Then Juman continued with his story. I was keen to know what the medicine man had done to them.

'Well, he examined us', Juman continued. 'Then he asked us to tell him where the pain was. Next, he chewed up a wad of betel nut and spat it at the place of the pain, at the same time talking to the spirit of the sickness. Then he did a strange thing.' Juman stopped for a moment and adjusted the little oil lamp that lit up his anxious face. He needed time to think, or perhaps to put his experience into words that I would be able to understand.

'This medicine man then got a stone jar and poured some water into it. Before putting a cloth cover on it, he asked me to look inside. I could only see water. He then began some incantations, speaking strongly to a spirit that only he knew about. He called it until he was sure the spirit had done what he wanted. Then he said, "Now lift the cover and tell me what you see in the jar".'

It had begun to rain. I bent over to hear more clearly what Juman was saying. He continued his story. 'Well, when I looked in the jar there was a thing inside it moving around and disturbing the water. I asked the man what it was. "That, my friend, is the spirit of the person who has given you this sickness. Beside the jar there is a long needle; take it if you wish. If you plunge it down into the water, you will kill the person who has put this evil sickness upon you."

' "But I don't want him killed, whoever it is," I said. "Just get him to take away the sickness that he has given us. That's all I ask."

' "Just as you wish", the medicine man replied, and concluded the performances with more mysterious hand movements and wizardry.'

It all sounded so weird. I knew that what Juman was saying was not just a flight of fancy. He was deeply in earnest.

'And were you healed, Juman?' I asked.

'Yes, from that time on we felt better and have had no trouble since.'

'But I think you *have* had trouble, both of you, Juman and Awing. If I'm not mistaken, your fellowship with the Lord has suffered. You have found it hard to pray and read the Bible. And I have noticed that there is a coldness in you now which wasn't there before. Is that not trouble, and trouble of a far worse kind than sickness of body? This is sickness of spirit.'

'It is all true what you say', replied Juman. 'And I want you to know that we still have four bottles of magic medicine which the medicine man gave us. We should get rid of them. Can I go and bring them up here now?'

BREAK FOR FREEDOM

While Juman was away I looked up some Scripture verses. How strange was this healing of body that had come to Juman and Awing. Yet it was their spiritual flatness that was most disconcerting.

Soon Juman reappeared, bringing the bottles. Two of them looked like bottles of water. Juman explained that the medicine man had breathed spirit power into them. They were to drink this if the sickness came back. The other two bottles were small. One contained a greenish substance and the other a yellow liquid that smelt like coconut oil. Both were for anointing.

'Are you sure that this is all the magic medicine that you have?' I asked. To keep back any would make futile any prayer for the Lord's help. We then read the Bible together —'Satan himself masquerades as an angel of light. It is therefore a simple thing for his agents to masquerade as agents of good.'

From Scriptures like this we learned that even Satan has the power to heal the body and to evoke lying wonders. But his chief aim is to cause alienation from God and the destruction of the spirit of all those who yield to his forms of magic.

We read other Scriptures together as a foundation for

their confession to the Lord, and to reassure them of His love and forgiveness.

Then, at about 9.30 that evening, Juman and I walked together to the edge of the river. It was raining and the river roared below us as Juman uncorked each of the bottles and threw them one by one right out into the swirling waters.

Guidelines

Disguise

'... for even Satan disguises himself as an angel of light' (2 Corinthians 11.14b RSV).

Separate

'... what harmony can there be between Christ and the Devil? ... And what union can there be between God's temple and idols? For you are God's temple, the home of the living God ... That is why the Lord has said, "Leave them ... don't touch what is unclean, and I will welcome you"' (2 Corinthians 6.15–17 Living Bible).

Talkback

1 *Assurance* What Scriptures would you use in re-assuring Juman and Awing of God's loving concern for them? (Psalm 103.8–14; Isaiah 40.27–31; John 14.1; Hebrews 4.15–16.)

2 *Wizardry* Does the Bible give illustrations of pagan practitioners with magic powers? (Exodus 7.8–12; Matthew 7.22–23; 2 Thessalonians 2.9–10; Revelation 19.20.)

3 *Discernment* In view of Satan's ability to deceive people by false signs and wonders, what tests may we apply in determining whether a person's 'special' experience is a true work of God or otherwise? (Matthew 7.15–16, 20–23; John 13.34–35; Galatians 5.22–25.)

4 *Antipathy* What Scriptures describe God's abhorrence

of false gods and occult paraphernalia among His people?
(Exodus 34.12–17; Deuteronomy 18.9–14; Revelation 21.8.)

Avoid the occult like the plague

'Be very, very careful never to compromise . . . for you must
worship no other gods, but only Jehovah, for he is a God
who claims absolute loyalty and exclusive devotion' (Exodus
34.12a, 14 Living Bible. See also Deuteronomy 18.9–14).

Occult (Latin: occultus, past participle of *occultere*, to cover
up, hide) . . . pertaining to, concerned with or designating
alchemy, magic, astrology and other arts and practices
involving use of divination, incantation, magic formulae,
etc. (*Webster's Collegiate Dictionary*).

PART THREE

If you accept and follow your spiritual master's
instructions, your life will become successful. If not, you
will miss the chance. Now, the choice is yours. He will not
compel you. He simply says, "These are my instructions.
You may act upon them or not, as you choose."

Make Your Life Successful

RARE DELICACIES

What about some of the way-out things that may be given you in Borneo? Baby bees? When cooked they are nicer than you'd think. Python? That tastes something like greasy, firm-fleshed fish. Or crocodile?—not unlike shark meat. If the worst comes to the worst you could always make soup of the crocodile's tail.

Make Soup of the Crocodile's Tail . . . 12

12 Make Soup of the Crocodile's Tail

'Look dear, what I've got in my soup. It's a chicken's leg!'

'That's not a chicken's leg, dear; that's its beak.'

'Oh, help!'

'Hush dear, our friends will hear you. Just keep calm and eat up; you're doing fine.'

My wife was new to the longhouse situation. However, it did not take her long to learn the right things to do and to appreciate the simple hospitality of the people.

What kinds of food would you find in a Bornean village?

The vegetable plot and the jungle are the tribesmen's supermart from which he gathers much of the greens and meat. The domestic fowl and village pig help bolster these resources, but are usually not killed except for special occasions such as feasts or for entertaining guests.

The folk feel that friendships are forged around a meal. They say that they don't really know a person until they have eaten with him. That is why on some occasions you are invited to eat with practically every family in a village.

In keeping with the tribal tradition of giving the best to visitors, missionaries are often given chicken meals. These chickens are usually the bantam-type village fowl; dainty little birds that scavenge around the compound and have a very definite pecking order of superiority. I sometimes wonder if they anticipate missionary visits with fear and trembling.

FARM MAKING

The life of the Bornean tribesman centres largely around his rice farm. He wants to be sure at least of his daily bread. Tribal villages are usually emptied during farm-making time, except for a few grannies and their smaller grandchildren. Every able-bodied person is called to muster for the hard work of cutting back the forests and tall grasses to make new rice plots.

Before he can farm in earnest, the animist has first to seek the favour of the spirits. He has to have the right omen. He will watch for the right movements of the fish hawk. The barking deer is an animal of sinister significance to some spirit worshippers, and should it bark within ear-shot of these farm workers their plot has to be abandoned—a frightful blow to folk living on the poverty line. But who dare defy a message from the spirits?

If all goes well, the rice will come to a head in five or six months, when the farmer will have to begin watching for jungle intruders; the deer, monkeys and finches that emerge in due season to share the crop. To ward off these pests, the folk construct some ingenious animal and bird-frightening contraptions—bamboo clappers, tin cans on strings, spinning windmills and gaudy cloths that flutter like ghosts in the breeze.

Harvest time is one of great elation. Everyone goes wild over the first-fruits of the rice, which they love to share with you. It has a special nutty flavour. The first days of harvest are times of much happiness and festivity. The Christians gather to thank God. They remember the old days of being deprived of their rice through pagan taboos. What a change Christ has made, even to their farming!

VARIETY A-PLENTY

You couldn't talk about Bornean food without a word on fish. They are an excellent addition to a limited larder and are always to be had. The folk catch them by line or by a large, hand-thrown net that does wonders in the shallower reaches. They also use a gill-net that is suspended by floats.

But if you really want to see the fish hauled in, the place for you is the fish-poisoning festival. In this, the tribes-people beat out the sap from a poisonous vine. This sap is then thrown into the river, stupefying all the fish within its reach for a distance of a mile or two. The folk some-times get enough fish to last them weeks by this means. They have to smoke it over their fires, of course, to preserve it.

Practically all jungle creatures are deemed good for food. Meat of a rarer order, edible but not so common, is that of the clouded leopard, the honey bear, scaly anteater or large lizard, all of which can be made tasty when cooked up with a little pig fat.

In these days in Borneo you need have little fear of coming to an untimely end through unpalatable food, though there may be times when you will be given rice and salt for dinner. It's all your host has. But the fellowship will be great.

How true are King David's words: 'Thou preparest a table before me in the presence of my enemies.' One thinks of travelling amid such enemies as tiredness, hunger and sometimes sickness, and of God's provision right out of the blue.

We had arrived at one longhouse, a rather poor community, feeling the fatigue of some hard river travel. As we clambered out of our longboat and up the river bank, I thought to myself: 'Yes, we're hungry. But these poor folk will have nothing to give us.' I'd greatly underestimated God's loving care for us. We could never get beyond His reach. Barely had we sat down on the splitboard verandah, than an angel arrived with a tray of papaya and bananas. A tribal angel of course, but nonetheless a messenger from the Lord as far as we were concerned.

What about some way-out things that may be given you in Borneo? Baby bees? When cooked they are nicer than you'd think. Python? That tastes like greasy, firm-fleshed fish. Or crocodile?—not unlike shark meat. If the worst comes to the worst you could always make soup of the crocodile's tail!

You must not be shocked if while shopping at an Asian meat market you are confronted by the head, hooves and appurtenances of a buffalo, cow or pig dangling over a gory assortment of meat. If you intend buying here, it would be best to ascertain first whether the meat has been ritually offered to the butcher's idols. This ceremony the butcher performs by murmuring a prayer as the first blood flows from the slain animal. Many Asian Christians are careful not to buy such meat.

ASIAN COURTESY

In true Asian fashion, the tribespeople prepare for a meal by spreading out clean mats on the floor where the food dishes will be placed and the folk sit. The meal is usually a one-course affair with rice as the mainstay, accompanied by some meat, greens or possibly noodles.

Time would fail me to tell at length about such things as *jarok*, a name given to salted fish or meat which is preserved in bamboo containers and kept for weeks or months. It often looks thoroughly decomposed when it is given you, yet the aura of mystery that surrounds it will have you agreeing with your host that he is giving you something of special vintage.

In the mainstream of missionary work, your attitude to the taking of food with Asians can speak louder than your sermons. Isn't it interesting that Christ used the symbol of fellowship around a food table to denote a oneness with Him in the purpose of His coming into this world?

A Bornean pastor was overheard talking about a missionary to some of his flock. 'It must be true what he says', the pastor remarked, 'he eats our food !'

Guidelines

Memo from Paul

'. . . . whatever a person is like, I try to find common ground with him so that he will let me tell him about Christ and let Christ save him' (1 Corinthians 9.22 Living Bible).

Talkback

1 *Distinction* Do you think it could be wrong in one culture to eat certain foods and right in another? (1 Corinthians 8.4–13; 10.18–33.)
2 *Broadminded?* Should a missionary have a care for the scruples of those among whom he is working, or should he try to 'broaden out' the folk to embrace his own views

on matters of meat and drink? (1 Corinthians 8.13; Romans 14.1–3, 15–21; 15.1–2.)

3 *Life-style* Could a missionary's life-style affect his witness in another land? (Ezekiel 34.1–6; 1 Corinthians 9.22–23; 1 Peter 5.1–3.)

4 *The overcomers* Do you think God can help us to overcome our pet aversions? (Philippians 4.10–13, 19.)

. . . But even so . . .

'. . . I can do everything God asks me to with the help of Christ who gives me the strength and power. But even so, you have done right in helping me in my present difficulty' (Philippians 4.13–14 Living Bible).

THE SCRIPTURE PICTURE

One day, the district officer, a European, arrived ... and called for his host ...

'Lian, ahm, about this picture that you have here among the government notices. I presume you put it there?'

'Yes, sir.'

'Lian, it's a bit different from government notices, don't you think?'

'Yes, sir.'

'Well, Lian, could I ask you to take it down. Those flames give me nightmares ...'

The Two Ways ... 13

'That looks good', said Agong as he drew back and took a long look at the picture he had just pinned to the outside wall of his room. The wall faced the longhouse verandah.

'Everybody will see it', he mused, as he put his head to one side and then to the other, viewing his new wall decoration, first wide-eyed and then with eyes half shut.

Agong was the headman of a pagan village. He hoped his picture would at least show where his heart lay. He admired the Christians. Pity his people didn't all feel as he did. But he'd wait. They'd catch on soon.

He spent what time he could in telling folk the meaning of his picture. It was the TWO WAY chart.

The broad way had many, variously-occupied travellers on it. Some were walking. Some were trading. Some were drinking. Some were fighting. A group up one end was squabbling over some cards while another cluster of folk was beating gongs and dancing. All very Eastern, except for the flames that enveloped the road's end.

The narrow way was an uphill road. It had a Cross at its gate and led to a land of brightness. Very few travellers were on it. A man with a book in one hand and the other hand raised imploringly leant over the dividing wall, inviting travellers to come through a little gate marked 'Life'.

'I got this from a Christian teacher', Agong explained to his village folk. 'And if you want to know where we are on this picture, this is us here, right in the centre of the broad way that leads to destruction. We've got to change or these flames here will have us for fuel . . .'

But Agong was very disturbed a few days later to see his picture torn at one end. He called the children together in a hurry.

Who's responsible for this', he queried, pointing to the tear in his picture. The children replied with looks of angelic innocence . . . 'Well, the first child I catch interfering with it will feel the strength of my mouth. I'll fine him.' Who could tell? The Christians' God was a very high and powerful one. He might well get angry and send a rebuke to reward such sacrilege, Agong pondered.

A lot of tribal folk are praying for Agong and his village, that God will open their eyes.

THE TRADING CENTRE

At the government centre further downstream another man, Lian, had pinned one of these pictures to the wall of the trading centre where he was the man in charge. He had framed it with neat bamboo strips to give it a little extra status. Folk were soon asking what it meant. Its message flowed easily into Lian's language and thought patterns. He was a Christian.

The variety of activities of the people characterized in the picture, plus the presence of a long, wide-mouthed snake lying along the wall that skirted the broad road, all added interest to it. Visitors to the trading centre often stopped to gaze at it, trying to work out its imagery. Then Lian would take over and drive home its message. Many of the visitors went away with long thoughts. Some would become Christians, Lian hoped.

One day the district officer, a European, arrived to stay overnight at the trading centre. Lian noticed him taking particular interest in his picture, and the more so as it was grouped alongside a number of government notices that Lian had been given for promulgation. In the morning the officer called for his host and spoke to him in a kindly way.

'Lian, ahm, about this picture you have here among the government orders and notices. I presume you put it there?'

'Yes, sir.'

'Lian, it's a bit different from the government notices, don't you think?'

'Yes, sir.'

'Well, Lian, could I ask you to take it down. Those flames give me nightmares...' Lian obeyed. But he kept it handy and was ready to use it with anyone who would listen.

Shortly after this, the same district officer arrived at

the village where our mission house was. He came around for a cup of tea, and on seeing the same offensive picture adorning our verandah wall his voice suddenly became abrasive.

'Ahhhm. Another of these, eh? Saw one at the trading post. The jolly thing gave me the creeps. Haven't you missionaries got something better to offer than these lurid drawings?'

I explained that the picture did not originate in the West. It was an Asian depiction of the Gospel message as presented by Jesus in Matthew 7.13. He looked perplexed and offended. We found out later that he had other reasons for disliking the Gospel. He loved the rice beer which the Christians had newly refused to make.

Sometimes there are 'other reasons' for our 'righteous indignation', aren't there? The devil doesn't mind what they are as long as we keep heading right along the broad way that leads to destruction. Many Borneans have seen the light through these Two Ways pictures and have veered to the narrow way that leads to life.

Guidelines

None so blind ...
'No wonder you grope like blind men and stumble along in broad daylight, yes, even at brightest noontime, as though it were the darkest night! ... For your sins keep piling up before the righteous God, and testify against you' (Isaiah 59.10, 12 Living Bible).

'Master, let me receive my sight' (Mark 10.51b RSV).

Talkback

1 *East is East?* Do you think that God's standards for Christians in the East are different from those He has for

Christians in the West? (Acts 17.25–28; Romans 3.9–26; 5.12; 10.12–13.)

2   *Threat*   A pagan chief threatens action against a church group if they will not stop preaching that hell is the end of the ungodly. The church asks your advice. What counsel would you give? (John 3.16–21; 2 Corinthians 4.1–6; 5.14–15.)

3   *Presentation*   What teaching would you give on avoiding offence in presenting the good news? (2 Corinthians 4.1–2; 5.14–15; Titus 2.7–8.)

4   *Partner*   What is the Holy Spirit's part in the communication of the good news. What effect should this knowledge have upon us in our speaking for Christ? (Acts 1.8; John 16.8–11; 1 Thessalonians 1.4–6.)

Not just meaningless chatter

'. . . when we brought you the Good News, it was not just meaningless chatter to you; no, you listened with great interest. What we told you produced a powerful effect upon you, for the Holy Spirit gave you great and full assurance that what we said was true' (1 Thessalonians 1.5a Living Bible).

TURBULENCE

'Hold on fellows, this is it', shouted Jim as we suddenly found ourselves enveloped in a wicked, bone-shaking turbulence that tossed us around like a cork. Visibility was nil. The battle was on. Lord, help us. No one else could . . .

Low Flying . . . 14

'Good trip in, Jim?' I asked the pilot as he unstrung a bundle of mail and books that he had brought in for some local churches.

'Oh, not bad as they go', he replied casually, 'though I never relish coming in over that ridge.' He nodded in the direction of a mountain range behind him, notorious for the mourning veil of dark cloud it wore through much of the day.

'And from the look of things, we'd best keep moving if we want to get through the Belaga gap before it closes', he added.

How glad we were to see the little plane appear on the horizon as it came in to that rugged interior spot to pick us up. Our aircraft had a great reputation for being just where you needed it. We always greeted the pilot with open arms, not only glad to see him personally, but excited at the prospect of getting back to our families after about three weeks away.

But I'd had a premonition on this particular day that something was going to go wrong. I couldn't help thinking that it was the Lord trying to warn us to be especially prayerful about the flight that we were about to make.

Why all this need for caution and care? I think it was because we had spent much of the past week in dealing with a demon-influenced man. Would the devil now try to strike back at us? Things like this did occur. We quickly stowed our baggage in the rear compartment of the aircraft and then boarded. Jim prayed for the Lord's hand upon our flight.

We were soon circling over the airstrip area to gain height before tackling that hole in the gap which had mercifully widened a little, exposing a magnificent patch of blue. Then Jim, with his keen eye for a free plane-wash, made for an orphan shower that quickly sped past after it had done its job.

On passing through the gap Jim surveyed the prospects

for a good two-hour flight back to base. Conditions seemed reasonable, nothing to chuckle about, but flying in interior Borneo rarely is. He then throttled back and got to work with his slide rule and knee pad to make a position report to the flight control centre on the coast.

'Say again your ETA', the operator's voice crackled through the speaker above our heads.

'I say again, ETA Lawas, zero five one five, zulu, over.' Jim replaced the mike to its holder on his left side and settled back to a more comfortable position in the pilot's seat. I was sitting beside him. Pastor Ajang had a full back seat to himself, which he seemed to be enjoying immensely. Great to be sailing over Borneo's jungles at 5,000 feet; a millionaire's life! The deer and the wild pig could have their forest tracks and the monkeys their tree tops. It was great up there with the eagles.

CLOUD BUILD-UP

I was dozing at the time when I noticed the wing lifting a little as Jim eased the plane through a slight course correction. Catching my waking eye he offered an explanation.

'Can't say that I like that build-up gathering over the Baram. Think we'll head out towards the coast. Things look better there.' In my view things always looked better out towards the coast where the flatter country made for more predictable weather patterns. I felt much more comfortable floating over the coastal roads and small bazaar townships that offered other alternatives to being lost among the dark and trackless mountains.

But even on the coast the weather was deteriorating and as we came over the Niah township the pelting of hard rain made us glad of the stout cabin that sheltered us. Visibility worsened as we came within a mile or two of the sea to notice a long untidy stack of dark cloud opposing the plans we had for curling around that way. Jim turned back, casting a cautious eye at his fuel gauges. He again picked up the mike to make a report of proceedings that were now being monitored with increasing concern by flight control.

'. . . now proceeding to Miri. ETA Miri, zero four one zero . . .'

As we came back towards the Niah area, feeling the resistance of the increasing rain that pressed in upon us, Jim began casting around for a possible emergency landing spot. We couldn't go chasing around like this for long, chewing up valuable fuel.

Below us stretched the long, narrow finger of the Miri road, a welcome sight as it wove its way northwards amidst its canopy of trees. I think we were all beginning to sense that things were not going happily, and the desire to pray came very naturally. I looked back at Ajang. He looked white and troubled, not knowing quite what was going on as he saw Jim's constant handling of the microphone and his scannings of the landscape.

As we descended to 200 feet, Jim soon concluded that the narrow, gravel road below us was no place for a landing. 39 feet of wingspan is not something to be easily fitted down on to 45 feet of road, indecorously overhung by trees and telephone wires.

'Sorry, fellows', said Jim, turning apologetically to his passengers. 'I'm afraid we'll just have to press on through that pea soup to Miri. Any hills in among that lot that you know of?'

The soles of my feet were very damp with perspiration by this time. Poor Ajang looked sick. I was sorry for him as he could only sense the danger without being able to understand all that was going on. I'm sure that he had never prayed more fervently in all his life; I hadn't!

Feeling sure that there were no hills in the middle of the dark stuff ahead, Jim checked his map again before committing us to it. There was no turning back. I was beginning to smell the brimstone in all this and remembered the premonition I'd had that morning. The Lord would have to see us through. Hadn't He once rebuked a storm at sea when evil powers were bent on destruction?

BONE-SHAKING TURBULENCE

'Hold on fellows, this is it', shouted Jim as we suddenly found ourselves enveloped in a wicked, bone-shaking turbulence that tossed us around like a cork. Visibility was nil. The battle was on. Lord help us. No one else could.

Jim handled the plane well. We were all goggle-eyed in our scrutiny lest we should suddenly find an unmapped knoll coming in through the windscreen, or even the ungainly limbs of a forest giant. The little text the pilot had stuck to the control panel, 'Underneath are the everlasting arms', was now the most appropriate thought in the world. We seemed to be gasping for a break from this clammy black hand that was bent on our confusion. Why didn't the storm take on someone its own size? They called ours a light aircraft. This was heavy weather.

The rain now lashed down at us like the spray of a thousand bullets. Jim's hand trembled on the throttle. Our cries for the Lord's intervention in this elemental rough-and-tumble were battering Heaven's gates. And God heard. He had not forsaken us.

Ten minutes of this was quite enough. If the pastor and I had previously not known why pilots avoid dark clouds like the plague, we knew now. Better be a live dog than a dead lion!

Suddenly a break in the clouds appeared and there, 100 feet below us, was a patch of large timbers butting their horns into the skyline. And beyond, a most welcome sight —the Miri road beckoning us on to the airport, safety and fuel, 30 miles ahead.

Our later arrival back at headquarters was just the usual type of aircraft return to base: the circling overhead, the final approach and touchdown to meet the welcoming hands and arms of wife and family. There are some things you don't like to talk about at the time.

A week or so later Jim received a letter from a friend 4,000 miles away asking, 'What was happening to you last Tuesday? We had a big burden to pray for you.' Jim checked the date. He knew only too well what had happened on that day. Things began to add up. This was a strong lesson to us on the importance of prayer.

Friend, let God pray through you. Someone may need your prayers today, more desperately than you will ever know.

MISSION FLYING IN BORNEO

Borneo is a rugged, jungle-covered country with few roads stretching into its interior. In ministering to the interior tribes aircraft have been a must for evangelism, Bible teaching, airlifting the sick to hospital etc. Our Mission began its flying programme in 1950 with a little Aeronca aircraft. The aircraft mentioned in the above story was a Helio Courier; a real workhorse for a tough job.

Time-saver! A journey that on one occasion took us 28 days travel can now be done by aircraft in 1½ hours.

Guidelines

Hand of prayer
'Whenever Moses held up his hand, Israel prevailed; and whenever he lowered his hand, Amalek prevailed' (Exodus 17.11 RSV).

Wonderful results
'The earnest prayer of a righteous man has great power and wonderful results' (James 5.16 Living Bible).

Talkback

1 *Hunches* Do you think Christians should take notice of hunches or premonitions? If so, what is a safe thing to do with them? (Proverbs 3.5–6; Philippians 4.6–7.)
2 *Trouble stirrer!* Can you recall any Scriptures that refer to Satan's stirring up the elements to trouble God's people? (Matthew 8.23–27.)
3 *Presumption?* Think of decisions made in critical

situations. At what point does a certain course of action
become—presumption? What Bible illustrations have we of
this? How should we pray for jungle pilots in this regard?
(1 Samuel 4.3–11; 13.11–13; Matthew 4.1–10; Psalm 27.11.)
4 *Safety* Where does the Bible link the safety of God's
servants with the prayers of the saints? (Genesis 18.22ff;
Exodus 17.8–13; Acts 12.5ff; Ephesians 6.12–13, 18–19.)

Safety is the Lord

'An horse is a vain thing for safety : neither shall he deliver
any by his great strength. Behold, the eye of the LORD is
upon them that fear him, upon them that hope in his
mercy' (Psalm 33.17–18 AV).

TELL ME

*An opening came when one of the village elders sat back
from his mat making . . .*

*'But tell me, when did all this happen about Jesus dying
on the Cross?'*

'About nineteen hundred years ago', I replied.

'About ninteen hundred years ago?' he questioned closer.

'Yes.'

*He thought for a moment while he worked something
out.*

*'Then if it is true as you say that we are lost without
this Jesus, surely you people wouldn't have waited all this
time to come and tell us.'*

Lockjaw . . . 15

'You are followers of God; we are followers of Bungan, the wife of God; therefore we are brothers.'

The village headman was trying bravely to be cordial. But his was a pretty desperate attempt. He knew so little about our faith.

We thanked him for letting us visit his village. After all, he could have sent us high-tailing it for home. From his point of view there was little he could gain from our visit except a few medicines. The old man gave us a benign smile and settled back hoping to collect some more words of comfort.

'But, sir, we beg your leave to point out that our religions are not the same. We come to tell you about the True God. We bring you news of a Saviour. We have a book which tells us the way of God.'

We continued our story amid the tangled noise of disagreeable dogs and fat-tummied children. A group of village leaders sat around the walls of the large longhouse room, chewing betel-nut and occasionally refilling their mugs with rice beer from a large basin.

The headman came in again. The fact that his religion had no book had always been a sore point with the younger generation in his village. 'Now, my sons, consider well', he continued. 'We haven't been given any book. We are the blind ones, if you like. But Bungan blesses us with rice for beer. We like beer, it loosens us up, my sons, it frees our spirits.'

There were wooden images, sacred groves and special offerings of eggs scattered around the village.

That's how far we got with this old headman. He died recently, a merry old soul, but lost! He never forbad our visits. He thought our religion could be good for those stalwarts, steel-willed and foolish enough to give up the liquor.

WHEN DID ALL THIS HAPPEN . . .?
In the afternoon we walked the length of one of the long-

houses to chat with the folk. The people were in a holiday mood. It was after-harvest time. An opening came when one of the village elders sat back from his mat making, blew shavings from a spot beside him and invited us to sit down. We told him the good news of Christ and of His death on the Cross to open Heaven's gate for us. He was an intelligent man and listened thoughtfully before coming up with a question.

'I've heard your words. They are good words', he said. 'But, tell me, when did all this happen about Jesus dying on the Cross?'

'About nineteen hundred years ago', I replied.

'About nineteen hundred years ago?' he questioned closer.

'Yes.'

He thought for a moment while he worked something out. 'Then, if it is true as you say that we are lost without this Jesus, surely you people wouldn't have waited all this time to come and tell us?'

'And what about my parents and ancestors? They can't be really lost if they've never even heard this message of Jesus which you bring.' It seemed incredible to him that such a life-and-death story should have had to wait so long for its telling. It just couldn't be true!

It was a hot day and we had a long paddle back up-river in an open canoe—plenty of time for the old enemy to rub in the implications of this pagan's rebuff. It went into our system like salt into an open wound.

THE VISITOR

Not long after this, some folk from this pagan village arrived at our mission house carrying a sick man on a pallet. I glanced down at him and then at my wife. We were aghast. It was the village elder who had questioned us. He was desperately ill. A tetanus germ had got into one of the sores on his foot and the tell-tale signs of lockjaw had begun to creep over his face. My wife treated him and we prayed much over him, bidding him to turn to Christ. But he did not.

He lay propped up against a friend's shoulder.

'Hold on, fight it, fight it', his friends yelled in his ear, as they bade him resist death and hold on to the last breath of life in his body. Some women were trying to force some rice between the clenched teeth of his locked jaw, but most of the food dropped down on to his neck. He was in a lather of perspiration, putting up a hard fight. But before long the eerie wail of pagan crying told us that the battle was over. He'd gone to join his ancestors.

'That's his fate', said one of his friends as we talked later. Pagan folk try hard to take death in their stride but don't make much of a job of it. It is still a fearful spectre that taunts and terrifies them at inopportune moments.

Is it any wonder that the fear of death is upon them, since the sentence of death is upon every man outside the shelter of Jesus' cross?

Question : What am I doing to bring Christ's offering of Life to those who are under the shadow of death?

Guidelines

Human harvest

'Look around you! Vast fields are ripening all around us, and are ready now for reaping ... What joys await the sower and the reaper, both together!' (John 4.35b, 36b Living Bible).

Talkback

1 *Any hope?* Would you have held out any hope to this man for his ancestors who died without hearing the good news? (Genesis 18.25b; John 3.3; 17.3; Acts 4.12.)

2 *Lost* 'If the heathen are lost, it is not because they are unevangelized but because they are sinful men', says a writer. Does this accord with Scripture? (Isaiah 53.6; 64.6; Romans 3.9–12; 23; Ephesians 2.3–5.)

3 *Top priority* In what terms does God place great

urgency upon the proclamation of the good news? (Ezekiel 3.16–19; Matthew 18.12–14; John 4.35–36; James 5.20.)

4 *Privilege* Why should we deem it an immense privilege to be ambassadors of God in carrying the royal news of life to those under sentence of death? (Daniel 12.3; Luke 19.16–17; John 15.15–16; 2 Corinthians 4.17; James 5.20.)

God's stars

'And those who are wise . . . shall shine as brightly as the sun's brilliance, and those who turn many to righteousness will glitter like stars forever' (Daniel 12.3 Living Bible).

WHO'S THERE?

. . . My wife and I decided to pop over to the scene of Helen's dilemma to try and get a clue on the mysterious noise.

'Does it occur at the same time each night?' we asked.

'Yes, it seems to come about the middle of the night.'

'Ever thought of getting up to see what it's all about?'

'Too scared!'

Noises in the Night . . . 16

'Want to know something?' said Helen as she leaned over our gate. 'We've got a noise in our house.'

'What kind of noise?' I asked.

'It comes at night', she replied with a little grin. 'Shakes the whole place.' In spite of her smile, I could see that she was disturbed.

'But tell me, is it a banging noise or what does it sound like?'

'Well, it sounds like somebody walking about with a heavy tread, enough to shake the whole house. Joan and I are getting a bit edgy. Got any ideas?'

Joan and Helen lived in the upstairs portion of a nice house just across the airstrip from us. When we heard of their predicament we wondered if they were having night visits from pranksters, or were there really ghosts? Neither of them were sleep-walkers, they said.

Then we thought of the little barking lizard that lived in their rafters. Could that have anything to do with it? We often heard its bark at night but apparently *it* never worried the girls. But what was this other thing?

In our early days of missionary life we often have problems with unfamiliar sights and sounds. I was told before arriving in Borneo that pythons made a whispering sound as they moved. I decided that I'd watch out for that whispering sound. Thus the first few nights of my life in Borneo were marred by a python patrolling the palm-leaf roof of my quarters. Those whispering sounds in the rafters simply gave its game away. The unsatisfactory thing was that it could disappear so quickly when I switched on my torch.

But Helen had a real problem, a matter of night noises. It so happened that I was a little nervy about night noises myself at that time, having just returned from a trip to the interior, in which we'd been involved in some weird goings-on at a border village. Evil spirits were about, I was told, throwing sticks and stones at night and bashing at people's doors.

The man of the house where I was staying was deeply distressed, saying that they had been awakened several nights by a fierce bashing noise at the door. It wasn't the usual scraping of a stray dog but something far more sinister. It made me tremble too when I heard it at about three in the morning, one of a number of strange events that were making the whole village jumpy. We had special prayer about it, asking the Lord to rebuke the devil who was so obviously mixed up in this frightening business.

THE INVESTIGATION

Was it Socrates who said, 'I cease to fear that which I have examined'? My wife and I decided to pop over to the scene of Helen's dilemma to try and get a clue on the mysterious noise.

'Does it occur at the same time each night?' we asked.

'Yes, it seems to come about the middle of the night.'

'Ever thought of getting up to see what it's all about?'

'Too scared!'

'Well, what about both of you making an agreement that if the noise occurs again tonight you'll both jump out immediately and challenge the thing?'

But then we thought: what if one chickens out and leaves the other to the investigation?

'Rats? Do you have rats in your ceiling?' I asked further.

'No, what do you think the barking lizard is there for? And we've got a cat too, remember?'

A cat! Yes, we did remember and something suddenly began to click into place. Mooty, their cat, was a benign old Siamese, the oldest feline on the compound and very heavy on his feet.

'Where does Mooty sleep at night?'

'On the fridge', Helen replied. 'He likes the warmth from the kerosene-lamp chimney at the back.'

'Does Mooty scratch himself much?'

'Yes, he deals with his itches in the usual way.'

We walked over to the fridge and looked at the spot

where the cat slept. I then put both hands on to the fridge and gave it a little rock, similar in motion to what a cat might cause in scratching itself.

'That sounds like the noise', said Helen as she watched me. 'Well, you wouldn't believe it!'

We settled down for the night, thankful to the Lord for showing us the answer to a worrying problem.

Guidelines

No anxiety

'Don't worry about anything, but in all your prayers ask God for what you need, always asking him with a thankful heart. And God's peace, which is far beyond human understanding, will keep your hearts and minds safe, in Christ Jesus' (Philippians 4.6–7 TEV).

Talkback

1 *Little things* Has the Bible anything to say about Christians helping one another in little things. In the light of John 13.34 how significant is such help? (John 13.1–5, 12–15, 34–35.)

2 *Cats* In problems where spirit activity is suspected should we first look for a natural cause? (Mark 6.48–51.)

3 *Unnatural* What counsel would you give to Christian tribesfolk alarmed by violent noises and occurrences that had no natural explanation? (2 Corinthians 10.4–5; Ephesians 6.11ff; 2 Thessalonians 2.9–11; 1 Peter 5.8–9.)

Victory over Satan

'Our brothers won the victory over him by the blood of the Lamb, and by the truth which they proclaimed; and they were willing to give up their lives...' (Revelation 12.11 TEV).

'BUT NOW WE KNOW...'

'*What would have happened if you had ignored the message from the barking deer ...?*'

'*Ah*', he replied, '*it is hard for you to understand. We had learned by hard experience that when we ignored such warnings disaster overtook us. It was a costly thing to ignore the spirits.*

'*But now, we know that Jesus is more powerful. How do we know that? We prove it time and again when we disobey any and all of the old omens that used to bind us ...*'

Who Believes in Evil Spirits? ... 17

17 Who Believes in Evil Spirits?

'Oh, Lord Jesus, you are responsible for us now. You protect us.' A great, wooden idol had come crashing to the ground and the people were afraid. Would the evil spirits take revenge with some plague or disaster? Was this Jesus strong enough to protect them as the missionary had said? Very pertinent questions, indeed! This occurred at a tribal village on the day that they turned to Christ.

Do you believe in evil spirits? You probably wouldn't have read this far if you didn't. But some folk don't. They think that when Jesus and His disciples referred to demons and evil spirits they were merely playing to the superstitions of the Jews.

But we cannot dismiss the plain language of Scripture just like that. Nor can the evil-spirit experiences from foreign lands be brushed off so easily.

For a start, the New Testament states that the world is Satan's roving ground. What do you make of such Scriptures as these?:

'The whole world is in the power of the evil one' (1 John 5.19b RSV).

'While (the boy) was coming, the demon tore him and convulsed him. But Jesus rebuked the unclean spirit, and healed the boy . . .' (Luke 9.42 RSV).

If you live in a Christianized land you will not be so conscious of demon activity, because you do not see it in its blatant forms. I think that a certain missionary to Indonesia was right on the ball when he wrote:

'In the heathen world, still untouched by the Gospel, there are dark, spiritual powers at work which we in Christendom know nothing about . . . the heathen are exposed to many influences from the kingdom of darkness from which we seem protected.'[1]

[1] *The Living Christ and Dying Heathenism* by J. Warneck (Baker).

One of the first and greatest things that Jesus does when Bornean folk turn from their idols to the Christian Way is to break the iron yoke of demon oppression. What do we mean by demon oppression? My experience is that pagan people live in a weird and tyrannical world controlled by forces they fear and little understand but are always trying to come to terms with.

'. . . and we abandoned that rice farm . . .' said Uning as he concluded a story of pagan days.

'But what made you abandon that rice farm?' we asked.

'Because we heard the warning noise of the barking deer, a message from the spirits to say that we had offended them . . .'

This was a typical story of a kind that tribesfolk often relate. But then we asked Uning the obvious question :

'What would have happened if you had ignored the message from the barking deer and stayed on that rice farm?'

'Ah', he replied, 'it is hard for you to understand. We had learned by hard experience that when we ignored such warnings disaster overtook us. It was a costly thing to defy the spirits. But now we know that Jesus is more powerful. How do we know that? We prove it time and again when we disobey any and all of the old omens that used to bind us.'

Have you heard how the Murut people of Borneo were converted to the Christian faith? They were one of the most decadent tribes in the land. Drunkenness, lethargy and evil-spirit bondage were written right across their history. How were they changed? Does this letter from the (then) Rajah of Sarawak to the Borneo Evangelical Mission throw any light on the subject?

'I am amazed at the change in the Murut tribe. They used to be notorious drinkers but when offered whisky the other day they refused . . . It's remarkable, remarkable . . . I believe you have done more good in a few years than the Government has done in forty. Yet, the thing that surprises me is that your Mission does all this by methods of faith and spiritual means . . .'

RETURN TO PAGANISM

But let us have a look at the subject in reverse. What happens when Bornean folk deliberately turn back from the Christian Way to Satan? Some sinister form of spiritual upheaval is bound to occur. This was the case with a tribal couple contacted recently. They, with the rest of the village had turned to the Lord as their protector. Being illiterate, the learning process for them was a slow one.

Before long, it seems that they were confronted with a sickness. Against the advice of their elders they chose to consult a witchdoctor instead of resorting to prayer. There had been a number of miraculous healings in that area and so the power of Christ to heal was no new phenomenon.

But, in turning to the witchdoctor at this particular time of spiritual sensitivity in the village, they overlooked one thing: that in turning back from Christ they were opening themselves to something beyond their control. They became demon possessed.

These were ordinary village folk not given to any mental abnormalities or direct contact with Satanic powers. But now, they were taken over body and soul by a demonic invader and began running amuck in the village. Their yelling and restless wandering continued day and night with no one able to control them. Their children had to be taken from them and the whole longhouse was kept awake and on edge day and night.

'Let's call the witchdoctor and ask him to evict the demon', the village elders suggested in desperation. But the witchdoctor proved impotent. Meantime, the village folk were getting worn out by the wild performances. Few had slept for nights. Finally, the village deacons got together.

'It's true', they pondered, 'this couple has turned their backs on Jesus. But for the sake of us all, let us call on Him for help.'

They then gathered around the stricken pair. 'Oh, Lord Jesus', they cried, 'we are new followers of you. We are not clever at knowing what to say or do. But please have mercy on us all and save this couple from the wicked spirit.'

'And what happened then?' I asked.

'The couple soon quietened down and slept', their leader replied. 'And when they awoke they were better. Jesus' power is very great.'

On the strength of this, many folk asked to be baptized in the Name of this Jesus who had proved Himself so strong in freeing the demon-possessed couple. 53 were baptized on the Sunday afternoon of our visit.

How foolish and disastrous for anyone who has known the touch of Christ to flirt with powers that are hell-bent for chaos and destruction.

Guidelines

Be clean

'Go out from the midst of her, purify yourselves, you who bear the vessels of the Lord' (Isaiah 52.11b RSV).

Whose servants

'Do you not know that if you yield yourselves to any one as obedient slaves, you are slaves of the one whom you obey ... yield yourselves to God as men who have been brought from death to life ...' (Romans 6.16a, 13b RSV).

Jesus' power over Satan

'And whenever the unclean spirits beheld him, they fell down before him, and cried out, "You are the Son of God" ' (Mark 3.11 RSV).

Talkback

1 *Break* In his initial turning to the Christian faith, a pagan's break with his idols is a token of his turning from sin. Can you think of any Scriptural precedents? (2 Kings

11.17–18; 2 Chronicles 33.15–16; 1 Thessalonians 1.9–10; 2 Corinthians 6.16–18.)

2 *Regress* Why do you think Eastern churches consider lapses into idolatry and witchcraft sins of great gravity? (Deuteronomy 18.9–12; Exodus 32.1–6, 25–29; 2 Corinthians 6.16; 1 John 5.21.)

3 *Nemesis* 'That's why he's sick, he's committed some evil'—is a pagan attitude towards sickness and misfortune. What teaching should we give new Christians about this? (Genesis 3.16–19; John 9.1–3; Romans 8.21–23; Revelation 21.3–5.)

4 *Control* The Bible indicates that this world is lying passively in the devil's arms (1 John 5.19). What do you think this means? What response should this evoke in us, Christ's witnesses? (John 8.44, 36; 2 Corinthians 10.4–5; Hebrews 2.14–15; 1 John 3.8.)

True freedom

'... if the Son makes you free, you will be free indeed' (John 8.36 RSV).

PRAYER PLUS...

... The poor girl did look sick and had that vacant stare that tells you that other powers have been around. As we squatted down in the semi-darkness of the room, the father came out with that worrying statement, 'We'll be making a feast. Yes', he continued, 'we'll be getting in some provisions as soon as we can. She's been very ill.'

The talk about feasts was becoming epidemic...

How a Heresy Began ... 18

'Please come and pray for our sick baby', said the distressed mother.

It was a warm night. Pastor Amos and I were sitting on a seat outside a row of shops watching the world and his wife go by. Regiments of insects flocked around the pressure lamp that lit up the bazaar with all its gaudy array of cloths, pots, dried fish, outboard engines and general hardware. Many of the doorposts leant precariously, as this shopping block was old. Into one of the upstairs hovels Pastor Amos and I were called to pray for this sick baby.

There was a lot of sickness about when we were visiting this rather remote area. The Pastor and I were often called to the bazaar to pray with sick folk who had come from neighbouring longhouses to seek treatment at the local dispensary.

'I'm tired of these people', lamented the medical dresser. He seemed despondent about many of the cases and the constant battle against the filth and primitive conditions that existed in several of the local villages. He knew that even if he managed to cure some of the folk they'd soon be going back to the mud, the spit and the general squalor to be re-infected. Then there'd be the grouch about the weakness of the dresser's medicines. We felt as sorry for him as we did for the people.

We entered the tiny room where the sick infant lay. A string-wick lamp lit up the faces of the worried parents, a young tribal couple from a longhouse about three miles downstream. Over in one corner of the room was a pile of rubbish, the sordid residue of a score of other sick ones who had occupied the place. The mother gathered the child up into her lap.

'Pray for him', she said. 'He's sick. And tell God that we'll be making a feast later.'

'But why make a feast?' we asked.

'Well, we want to have special prayer later on. But we're not ready yet', she pleaded.

Pastor Amos and I were baffled about this business of making a feast. I didn't think that we were so far removed from tribal culture as to miss any hidden message. In any case we prayed and the next day the child had lost its raging fever and seemed much relieved.

THE FEAST IDEA AGAIN

Then we received another call. A tribal elder lay sick with a large lump in his groin. His folk had brought him up to another bazaar attic where he was being treated. I knew him quite well, a friendly soul whose strong professions of piety were always being betrayed by his fuzzy speech. He loved the rum bottle but on this day he was miserably sober. As Pastor Amos and I bent low to get through the door I noticed that the elder held a short, blunt stick which he was using to press against the lump to allay the pain. He wanted prayer.

'They'll be taking me home soon', he said. 'Then we'll make a feast and have special prayer.'

The feast idea again. What was going on? We immediately recalled that this man was from the same longhouse as the sick baby. The folk there had not long turned to the Christian faith and were still very untaught, a matter aggravated by the fact that they were of a very small tribe whose language none of us knew. Our contacts with them had been in the trade language, which proved so inadequate for communicating the truths of life and death.

The conundrum came around full circle when we actually visited the longhouse a few days later. If ever a place could dampen the morale and stifle the immortal spirit of man it was this one. It was filthy. Not long before they had had a score or more of captured wild pigs tethered to their longhouse verandah. They had caught them during a wild-pig migration in the area and were trying to fatten them. The place reeked.

AT THE LONGHOUSE

Old and rotten floorboards creaked and bent as we moved up the wide verandah that hadn't long been shorn of its evil spirit debris. Oh, to see just one flower edging the path of something beautiful, and all would be forgiven.

'There's a girl here who's being visited each night by an evil spirit', a deacon announced. 'It tries to kill her. She's terrified. You must come and pray.'

The poor girl did look sick and had that vacant stare that tells you that other powers have been around. As we squatted down in the semi-darkness of the room, the father came out with that worrying statement, 'We'll be making a feast. Yes', he continued, 'we'll be getting in some provisions as soon as we can. She's been very ill.'

The talk about feasts was becoming epidemic. A little red light began flashing wildly within us. Here was a good, old-fashioned heresy being spawned right under our eyes.

In their old custom, feast-making was a way of quieting offended spirits, a way of saying to the demons, 'Here, this feast is in your honour. Accept our offering and spare us.'

We prayed for the sick one. And that night we had a meeting on the longhouse verandah.

'Brethren', we said, 'please stop this feasting. It is the thin end of the devil's wedge. He'll not stop at asking feasts of you. Soon he'll be demanding blood sacrifices as he did in your old pagan custom. And you'll offer them out of compassion for your sick.'

Then we drew them back to the safety of Jesus' Name and His power over Satan, sickness and death. How subtle is this satanic stratagem, aimed at this almost defenceless people, untaught and vulnerable. We had much teaching to do regathering their hearts around the strong Name of Jesus and all that He had done for them.

Martin Luther once said : 'One error overthroweth the whole doctrine.'

Can you see what he meant?

Guidelines

Feasts won't help

'... your appointed feasts my soul hates; they have become a burden to me' (Isaiah 1.14 RSV).

128 One Way Through the Jungle

Look and live
'... John saw Jesus coming ... and said, "Look! There is
the Lamb of God who takes away the world's sin!" ' (John
1.29 Living Bible).

Talkback

1 *Error* What Christian doctrine did this feast-making
error 'overthrow'? (Romans 5.9; Hebrews 10.14; 1 Peter
1.18–19; Revelation 5.9.)

2 *Stress* What aspects of Christ's atoning work would
you stress in teaching the folk of this village? (Isaiah 64.6;
Ephesians 2.8–9; Hebrews 10.19–22.)

3 *Discernment* How important is the gift of discernment
to a missionary? Should he ask the Lord for this gift?
(1 Kings 3.7–10; Isaiah 11.1–4; Philippians 1.9–10; James
1.5–6.)

4 *A Flower!* Do you think it would be out of place to
give a little teaching on practical hygiene or the planting
of a flower or two to these folk? (Genesis 35.2–3; Numbers
8.6–7; Matthew 5.14–16.)

Know the difference

'Give me an understanding mind so that I can ... know
the difference between what is right and what is wrong. For
who by himself is able to carry such a heavy responsibility?' (1 Kings 3.9 Living Bible).

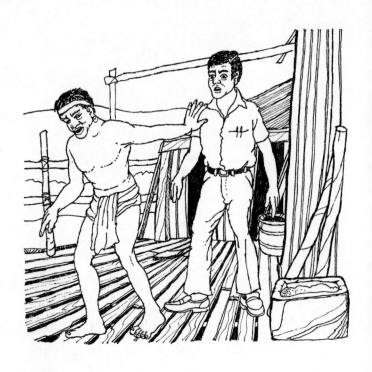

CUSTOMS AND CULTURE

... The old man spoke at length about the fish hawk as one of the most revered omen birds.

'But', I replied from my superior heights, 'don't you see that the hawk is just a mere bird that you could shoot with your gun and cook in your pot without any harm coming to you?'

The elder walked away in disgust, shaking his head.

'You do not understand, my son. You just do not understand.'

Cough and Come In ... 19

I heard the cough a hundred yards away when it was over in the rubber plantation that separated our house from the village. Then the tribesman coughed again, this time a hearty, throat-clearing roar as he crossed the little stream and came up the hillock to the house.

What do you think he was doing? Fighting back a sudden onset of bronchitis? Ah, no. In true Bornean custom he was 'knocking' from a distance to inform me of the approach of a friend. Then he emerged from the sticks.

As he climbed the notched pole on to our verandah he geared his voice down to a gentle 'Ahem' that signalled his presence outside my room. If I'd waited for him to knock on my door, I'd have waited in vain, for in his book he had knocked already and given me forewarning of his coming in his kindest terms.

'What is it, Liman?' I asked.

'I've come to see you', he said.

We first discussed the drought, and the farming and the prevalence of wild pig in the area. After ten minutes Liman came to the point.

'What do you think? Would you have some old tin cans to spare?'

'Sure, but why do you want old tin cans?'

'The deer have been at my farm, eating the *padi*. I want to string up a noise-making fence around the edge.'

I began saving old cans for Liman.

CUSTOMS AND CULTURE

If you come to Borneo to tell the Good News you will want to learn how the people tick over. The fact that we have crossed oceans to be missionaries does not mean that we will be acceptable people in another land. We have to earn our right to speak by sitting where the people sit, quietly listening, watching and learning their way of life. But even after many years we find there are things that we've skimped on.

One day we asked a Bornean friend to sit down and tell us of any things that he could think of that he found hard to take. We felt that we were just not clicking in some ways. Why not ask a Bornean friend to help us improve? It took him a long time to speak. You will find that Asian people are very gracious and most reluctant to appear the slightest bit impatient with their guests.

'Well', he replied, 'seeing that you've asked me and I know you very well, I'll perhaps tell you a thing or two. When we visit you, you sometimes leave us standing at the door while you talk with us. In our custom that is not good. We like to show our respect for visitors by inviting them right into our homes. We ask them to sit down so that we can talk things over in comfort. If the business is lengthy, we serve coffee.'

We wilted, thinking of the times we must have offended.

'And talking of coffee', he continued, 'we never ask a person if he'd like a second cup. In our custom we fill the visitor's cup again and again to assure him of our welcome.'

What are some other little things that indicate that we have done our homework? We will be aware that the folk are real people with feelings and susceptibilities very much like our own. We will remember that we are *guests* in *their* country and will have a keen sensitivity to the ways *they* do things. For instance, we will have learned to point with our chin rather than our finger—an impolite practice in the East. As Dr Nida points out in his book *Customs and Cultures* : if you do point with your finger and ask 'What is that', the folk might well reply : 'That is your finger !' Also, we will have learned to accept and offer things with our right hand, or better still, with both hands.

But what about learning the language of the people? Our diligence here tells the folk that we do really care, especially if we learn it in their homes and sitting places. Of course, we'll make mistakes that cause laughter and really pink up our cheeks. A missionary was telling the story of Abraham's offering of Isaac and wondering why her audience seemed mystified. She had used the wrong word and told the folk that Abraham had brandished a 'banana' to slay his son.

Sometimes we offend when we run down the religion of the folk we are trying to win. This is an awful mistake and one which we proud Westerners can easily make. I know because I did. It was while talking in my early days to an old pagan elder of animistic persuasion; that is, one who believes that the spirits send messages through birds, animals, rocks, trees, etc. The old man spoke at length about the fish hawk as one of their most revered omen birds.

'But', I replied, from my superior heights, 'don't you see that the hawk is just a mere bird and one that you could shoot with your gun and cook in your pot without any harm coming to you?'

The elder walked away in disgust, shaking his head. 'You do not understand, my son. You just do not understand.'

We've talked about the differences of custom. The culture of the Bornean folk is also very different and is in a state of constant change. Quite apart from the effect that the Good News is having on Bornean culture, the education explosion and such things as the effects of urbanization are causing great changes in the people's life style. Many are a little bewildered by so much, so suddenly.

How do we relate to these situations? We can show that the Bible is very relevant to *their* culture. It can speak to every man under the sun in his own language and cultural forms. We remember that Christianity was born in the Middle East and not the West as many might suppose, and that Jesus Christ took the nature of a servant in bringing us back to the Father.

CULTURE SHOCK
Do you know what culture shock is? When we move into cultural situations very different from our own, we can become badly shaken and disorientated. This sometimes happens to us Westerners going to the tribes. We are hit by the sheer ruggedness of tribal life. Some fellow-missionaries

working in a longhouse situation in central Sarawak recently wrote this in a letter to folk at home :

Disturbed nights Bed-bugs abound. Dogs! dirty, mangy, half-starved creatures, snarling and fighting. You have heard one dog howl? Have you heard 200 or so howl all at once? They seem duty bound to set up a chorus four or five times a night.

Poor diet Wild pig and fish are scarce; that leaves rice. (We take gifts for our hostess, but not food, as we find it gives the impression that we despise their food).

Heat It's bad anywhere, but in the old longhouses where the rooms are low, one boils slowly.

Bathing Lovely in the Akah, but in the muddiness of the Baram and Tinjar rivers, one wonders if one is cleaner before going in than when one comes out.

Privacy There is none. We are constantly under observation.

Medical work This has been quite heavy. Vomiting and diarrhoea are epidemic in some houses, while flu with the inevitable bronchitis and pneumonia is in others. Mosquitoes, sandflies, dirt and constant pressure of people and problems leave the flesh crying, 'Enough, enough!'

More families have turned to the Christian faith, but they need teaching. In every longhouse we met so many questions : 'Tell me the meaning of that last verse, child', one bent old lady requested. 'Why don't you stay longer?' 'When are you coming again?' 'We need teaching.'

IF YOU WISH TO BE A BLESSING
If there is one thing a pagan wants to hear, it is good news. He has had so much of the bad. Forgive me for using an illustration from another land, but it brings out the point so clearly. One of the first baptized Indians of Pennsylvania said this :

'I was a heathen and became old among the heathen, and am therefore well acquainted with everything about them. A preacher once came to instruct us, and began proving to us that there is a God. Then we said, "Why, do you think we do not know that? Return to where you came from." Again, a preacher came desiring to teach us: "You must not steal", he said, "nor drink, nor lie." We answered him, "You fool! Do you think we do not know that? Learn that yourself, and teach the people you belong to not to do so." ... After some time Charles Rauch came and sat down with me in my hut. The substance of what he said to me was this, "I come to you in the Name of the Lord of heaven and earth. He wants you to know that He would like to make you happy, and that He desires to lift you out of your present misery. For that end He became man and shed His blood for you."

'He went on thus, and then lay down on a board in my hut and fell asleep, for he was weary with his journey. Then I thought: "What sort of man is this? He lies there and sleeps so calmly. I could strike him dead, and throw him into the wood—who would make any enquiry about him? But he is not uneasy." I could not however get rid of his words. They recurred to me again and again, and even when I slept I dreamed of the blood which Christ has shed for us. Then, I thought this is something different, and I interpreted to the other Indians the further words which Charles Rauch spoke to us. Thus originated by God's grace the awakening among us. Therefore, I say to you: "Brethren, if you wish to be a blessing to the heathen, preach Christ to them, His blood and His death." '

Guidelines

Our attitude
'Let Christ Jesus be your example as to what your attitude should be. For he, who had always been God by nature,

[1] From J. Warneck's *The Living Christ and Dying Heathenism* (Baker)·

did not cling to his prerogatives as God's equal, but stripped himself of all privilege by consenting to be a slave and ... he humbled himself by living a life of utter obedience, even to the extent of dying ... (Philippians 2.5–8, J. B. Phillips).

Talkback

1 *Belief* What is animism? Does the Bible give us any light on it? (Romans 1.21–23; Psalm 96.4–5; 115.2–8.)

2 *Propaganda?* Why do you thing it is that some third world countries consider the missionary enterprise as propaganda for Western culture? What can we learn from this? What should we do about it? (Matthew 9.10–13; John 3.16; Acts 17.24–31; Galatians 3.28; Ephesians 2.11–13.)

3 *Culture* Has the Bible any guidelines for us in learning the culture of the people? (Ezekiel 3.15–17; 1 Corinthians 9.19–23; Romans 14.15–21; 2 Corinthians 4.1–5.)

4 *How far?* How far do you think a missionary should go in adapting to the culture patterns of the people among whom he is working, e.g. dress? If working among the tribes, should he adopt their dress? What principles should govern his conduct in this? (1 Corinthians 9.19–23; 14.20, 40.)

Winning their confidence

'When with the heathen I agree with them as much as I can, except of course I must always do what is right as a Christian. And so, by agreeing, I can win their confidence and help them too' (1 Corinthians 9.21 Living Bible).

ROCK BOTTOM

Entering the helicopter commander's office, I fumbled for my letter of introduction. The officer read it, looked up and stroked his chin. A frown crept over his brow. 'Look, sir, I see you have this letter of clearance. But I'm sorry, we have a flap on. Just can't take you ...'

Ajang and I moved off to downtown Sibu feeling at rock bottom. The convention was due to start within 48 hours, and we were separated from it by 200 miles of jungle and mountain.

Follow that Helicopter ... 20

'All aboard', the pilot called.

Pastor Ajang and I clambered aboard our Mission air-craft and strapped ourselves in. Then we prayed, com-mending our flight to God.

'Any complaints, men?' the pilot called over his shoulder.

'Right then, let's get rolling.' And away we shot, the engine at full bore as we chewed up 200 yards of airstrip and took to the air.

Pastor Ajang and I were due to visit a Christian con-vention deep in the interior, but we had foolishly run things late, leaving only two days to travel the 500 miles.

The first part of our journey was now under way. Look-ing down from the cabin of our aircraft I began to think of some of the uncomfortable alternatives to this kind of travel. There was the jungle below. I thought of the sweat and the climb, the leech-ridden tracks and mosquito forests. Then we edged nearer to the coast, reminding me of the boredom of slow-boat, coastal travel.

After three hours we were circling over Sibu airport waiting for a small army plane to land ahead of us. It was a time of intense communist activity in the area and the military were busy.

'Will you please park over near number one helicopter pad', the control tower called as we taxied in. Very appropriate, as we were banking on a helicopter ride for the next leg of our journey. Our own plane could take us no further than this coastal town. There was no airstrip at the deep interior village for which we were heading.

SETBACK

Entering the helicopter commander's office I fumbled for my letter of introduction. The officer read it, looked up and stroked his chin. A frown crept over his brow. 'Look, sir, I see you have this letter of clearance. But I'm sorry, we have a flap on. Just can't take you. Why not go to our next base at Long Tajam and try there?'

Ajang and I moved off to downtown Sibu feeling at rock bottom. The convention was due to start within 48 hours and we were separated from it by 200 miles of jungle and mountain. We hired a room, took a bowl of soup at a Chinese café and went into consultation.

At this time I was newly grateful to a good friend who had reminded me to 'give thanks for everything and especially when you are in a fix. It will help you see straight.'

Ajang and I decided to pray though our hearts felt frigid. We thanked God for the safe flight down to Sibu and for a place to rest. And we thanked Him for a lot of other things including the fix we were in, though He was not to blame. At times like these you realize that God is your only hope. Before long, we found our hearts strangely warmed. God was going to help us, we felt sure.

Hearing that there was a Chinese launch going upstream, we strolled along with our bags and boarded it for the night-long, 80-mile journey. It seemed full of people but not so full that it could not take on 23 soldiers who scrambled aboard five minutes before departure time. It was now 11 pm.

'I'll lie down here', said Ajang, making for a small vacant spot under a seat. He passed the night doubled up like a jack-knife. I curled myself around a luggage pile. We slept fitfully, reaching Kapit at eight in the morning. So far, so good. We thought a coffee shop would be a good place for considering our next move. Chinese coffee is always thick, strong and sweet and a good stimulant to early thoughts.

BY LONGBOAT AND 'CHOPPER'

We felt as we drank that the crowd thronging the sidewalks was God's raw material for His further use in our rescue. We were not mistaken. Out of that crowd, the Lord took a man called Kuda. He sped past the shop and doubled back. He'd seen us. We'd not seen him for years. My heart said, 'Thank you, Lord'.

'Why, you fellows will have a proper meal', he prophesied, and smartly ordered some rice and meat.

'Now, where are you bound for? I'm off in my boat to Long Tajam today. Can I give you a lift?' He was a quick-fire talker and talking our language.

Very soon, Kuda's boat was whipping us along to the next helicopter base where we arrived that afternoon. But there was still 100 miles to go to that convention village, with a wild range of mountains and many turbulent rivers yet to be travelled over.

At the helicopter base they were having a party. We were quickly swept into a smoky room filled with bottles and the clamourous singing of happy servicemen. Before long some bottled beer was placed before us, manhandled by a soldier with a bottle-opener. I parried for some soft stuff with which he obliged. But could he oblige with a helicopter?

'Look, sorry chaps. Can't help you', a naval lieutenant nearby replied. I smelt his breath and took courage in the thought that he might not be the final authority around here. 'Lord, he can't be!'

Going outside to the helicopter pads I spotted another officer, a man with whom I'd previously flown. He was now the commanding officer and greeted us most cordially. 'Yes, I've got chopper 'C for Charlie' going up to Long Dola this afternoon. But, I'd be obliged if you'd spend the night with us and take a less-loaded flight in the morning.' Were we dreaming? Yet, a touch of unbelief in me forbade immature exuberance. It still might rain!

The long flight over the mountainous no-man's-land was a rare delight. At times we ran into walls of cloud and just hovered while the helicopter pilot looked around for a hole. If it were not for the sturdy lapstraps I'm sure we'd soon have been flushed out of the cabin by the gale that blustered in through the open side door. We were now past the range and hiking along at river level, twisting and turning to follow the curling course of the river to our destination.

At about 10 am, one hour before the first convention

meeting was to begin, our Wessex helicopter 'G for George' settled down on its iron pad at the remote village of Long Dola.

Pastor Ajang and I have not forgotten the lesson we learned about praising the Lord in difficult circumstances. It seems to me that God works where His praises are. Surely, David the battle-scarred warrior of old had the secret when he declared : 'I will praise the Lord no matter what happens, I will constantly speak of his glories and grace' (Psalm 34.1, Living Bible).

Guidelines

Eagles' wings
'. . . they that wait for the LORD shall renew their strength, they shall mount up with wings like eagles, they shall run, and not be weary, they shall walk and not faint (Isaiah 40.31 RSV).

Talkback

1   *Praise*   What does the Bible teach us about praise to God as a weapon of great consequence in spiritual warfare? (Joshua 6.20–21; 2 Chronicles 20.21–30; Psalm 34.1–3; Acts 16.25–26; 1 Thessalonians 5.18.)

2   *Life lines*   How important are good communications to the carriage of the good news? (Isaiah 43.19; Acts 8.26–29.)

3   *Mixed blessing?*   Do you think that new roads and air routes into interior places could be a doubtful blessing in exposing remote people to the dissipations of modern civilization? What are the compensations? (Isaiah 9.2; 49.11–13; Matthew 28.18–20; Romans 10.15; 1 Thessalonians 1.8.)

4   *Authorities*   In the light of the Great Commission, how should we pray for 'kings and authorities' in receiving

countries? (Matthew 2.13–21; 1 Timothy 2.1–4; Proverbs 8.15–16; 21.1.)

Wonderful news

'This is wonderful news, and we aren't sharing it with anyone!... come on, let's go ... and tell the people ...' (2 Kings 7.9 Living Bible—read the whole chapter).

THE WITCH

. . . a woman broke through the door. She was a witch. Fresh pig's blood was dripping from her hands as she groped along the wall of the headman's room, placing gory hand-prints on the boards as she went. These were to protect from evil. She then smeared more pig's blood over her face.

Folk warmed to the thought that the spirit of Bungan would be pleased with her devotion and to hear her weird, ritual chanting, which soon increased to a kind of hysteria as she yielded herself body and soul to the spirit of Bungan for possession.

Happy Heathen . . . 21

'You know, these people are happy as they are. I don't
see why people should try to change them', said the young
European school teacher who was visiting a tribal longhouse
of Bungan worshippers.

Darkness was near as our longboat pulled in to the bank
for a nightstop at this pagan village. In the dim light we
could see a man slithering down the sticky river bank,
swaying wildly and clutching a little child in his arms. He
was bare-footed and bare-chested.

My heart went out to the child whose well-being seemed
threatened. Then one foot slipped and the man plunged,
child and all, shoulder first into the chocolate mud. The
rice beer had been too much for him. He got up again and
staggered to the river which was not too muddy to improve
his filthy condition.

Passing the variety of visiting canoes, we followed the
path of the drunk man up the bank. A frightened pig
grunted its disapproval as it darted off into the 'small bush'.
Some fowls fussed around as they went to roost. A spare
rooster, with callous disdain for lurking wild cats, perched
itself on a leafy branch overlooking the wooden catwalk
that we were now following.

As we approached the longhouse stairs we were almost
overcome by the stench of strong beer. Rotting *padi* husk
and some chewed sugarcane pulp carpeted the first steps.
Looking up into the longhouse we could see that there were
great goings on. A row of small kerosene lamps half lit the
faces of the tribesmen nearest the door, giving them a
strange wild-men-of-Borneo look.

'Any taboos on?' we enquired, feeling our way cautiously
up the slippery steps. We feared lest we should break faith
with these folk by interfering with an intricate pagan ritual
that seemed to be in progress. It could cost us a healthy
fine if we did.

'No taboos', a voice replied, 'you can come up.'

THE PAGAN FEAST

The dimly-lit longhouse verandah was alive with bodies. Unwelcome dogs darted here and there scrounging a rice cake in this room or a pig bone from the next, slinking away to enjoy the spoil in some quiet corner. Hungry dogs have no friends.

The rice beer was flowing freely as glassy-eyed stewards ladled it out of deep stone jars into rusty mugs. The sombre were getting talkative and the timid, brazen. Screams and raucous laughter preceded some half-clad bodies that lurched through a hide-hinged door and on to the verandah where we sat. Nearby, visitors began retching. The beer had character.

Beside us sat a group of betel-nut chewers, red-mouthed and communicative. They were not too choosey where they spat the overplus of red saliva that exuded from the messy wads in their mouths.

At this point I picked out the European school teacher, squatting, eyes agog, in the midst of a group of frolicsome youths. He looked entranced. He said he was new in the country and wanted to learn as much as he could about the ways of this fascinating people. The uninhibited rawness of the night appealed to him, as it well might while it was young, before the hangovers ripened, the drunken squabbles began and the swollen appetites of cavernous beer jars revealed what they had done to the year's rice crop.

'These people are happy. Why shouldn't we leave them as they are?' he asked of nobody in particular, but I could see that the question was meant for me. In this context I must have seemed to him like a fish out of water. We talked for some time until the wild screams of some girls made normal conversation impossible.

At one end of the verandah a crowd was gathering beneath the valiant beams of a pressure lamp. The slaughter of sacrificial animals had begun, and fresh blood was being sprinkled around in appropriate places for the spirits to see. The witchdoctors were in a mood for striking a hard bargain with their god as they called into the air :

'See, O spirit of Bungan, we are giving you blood, good blood, much blood. Hear us then. Keep us from disaster on the river, on the land. Give us life, long life, much *padi*, many children and plentiful riches. O Bali Bungan, do you hear?' The pathetic incantation rang out into the night air.

DEMON POSSESSION

Then a woman broke through the door. She was a witch. Fresh pig's blood was dripping from her hands as she groped along the wall of the headman's room placing gory hand-prints on the boards as she went. These were to protect from evil. She then smeared more pig's blood over her face.

Folk warmed to the thought that the spirit of Bungan would be pleased with her devotion, and to hear her weird ritual chanting which soon increased to a kind of hysteria as she yielded herself, body and soul, to the spirit of Bungan for possession.

Before long her prayer was answered and she passed into a trance, lying in a limp bundle on the floor. The watchers were delighted and a shout of triumph went through the longhouse. Bungan had come down. Folk greeted the Spirit Presence that now possessed the woman. A group of deep-voiced veterans then sang out a lengthy welcome with one man leading a theme and the rest joining in a chorus.

Nearby, the ritual wooden stand had been erected. As a contrast to the filth, the blood and stench around us, this stand was decked with fine things—sarongs, jungle knives, valuable beads and a variety of other tribal riches. In front of this there sat a man with a row of brass gongs before him, and a muffled gong-stick which he used to beat out a kind of uneven ting, tong, tong, for much of the ensuing night.

But what about the limp body of the witch lying there? At about eleven she was lifted up and the men took their turn waltzing her body around the stand of wealth, whilst the drunken choir with gong accompaniment chanted out an uncanny appeal to the Spirit Presence for more wealth and prosperity. This also went on for several hours. Sleep was out of the question for the worshippers, not so much because of the shindy but for fear of insulting the Spirit Presence.

Ever been glad to hear a cock crow? I have, often, and particularly at that time when the welcome note of stirring roosters announced the arrival of dawn and an end to the revelry.

The sun rose, inviting the fatigued worshippers to the forgiving waters of the nearby river. But there was no ready help for the sick heads and sore stomachs, and no panacea for the aching void. None?

The young school teacher moved off that morning holding a small C. S. Lewis book that I had given him. And the village resumed its life with a limp.

Happy heathen? Let the Westerner who despises his own birthright in Christendom come and imprison himself with the 'happy heathen' for a while, amidst the pain, the darkness, the fear, the filth and the injustice, and it may give him a better understanding of the pit from which he has been 'digged' (Isaiah 51.1). It could be that he will see what Jesus meant when He said: 'I am the light of the world; he who follows me will not walk in darkness, but will have the light of life' (John 8.12 RSV).

WHAT DO WE MEAN BY—'HEATHEN'?

'Heathendom', says Mildred Cable, one of a veteran missionary team to China, 'is not a low social condition, it is not poverty, it is not even an inferior code of morals. Heathendom is the condition of men whose worship is not directed towards God but towards Satan.'

'It is clear', says J. Oswald Sanders, 'that "heathen" may be found in the most polished society as well as in pagan degradation, for the point at issue is not social status but relationship to God.'

Taken from: *What of the Unevangelized?*, by J. Oswald Sanders.

Guidelines

Idolatry forbidden

'You shall have no other gods before me. You shall not make for yourself a graven image, or any likeness of anything that is in heaven above, or that is in the earth beneath, or that is in the water under the earth' (Exodus 20.3-4 RSV).

Worship whom?

'O worship the Lord in the beauty of holiness...' (Psalm 96.9 AV).

Talkback

1 *Happiness* What Scriptures show us that no one has the happiness of the heathen more at heart than God Himself? (Isaiah 55.5; Jeremiah 29.11; John 3.16; Acts 17.26-29; 2 Peter 3.9.)

2 *Heathenism* Would you say that heathenism is peculiar only to countries like Borneo? (Psalm 53.2-3; Isaiah 53.6; Romans 3.9-12; 1 John 1.8.)

3 *Idols* The Bible tells us to keep ourselves from idols. How would you describe an idol? Do you have any in your 'longhouse'? (Exodus 20.3-5; Psalm 115.4-8; Luke 12.15; Colossians 3.5b-6; 1 Timothy 6.17.)

4 *Prayer* To the pagan, prayer is not a matter of worship but of averting disaster. How does this differ from your view of prayer? (1 Chronicles 16.29; Psalm 95.6-7; 96.9; Luke 11.2.)

True Worship

'The one thing I want from God ... is the privilege of meditating in his Temple, living in his presence every day of my life, delighting in his incomparable perfections and glory' (Psalm 27.4 Living Bible).

SEARCH FOR LUCK

... 'Ah yes', said the headman, 'that was Naga, the river spirit. If we treat him kindly he will send us luck.'

But some of the longhouse folk thought the headman's reaction a very strange one. They didn't want to pay respect to Naga any more.

'We are Christians, aren't we?' they queried.

The River Monster ... 22

'I've had enough of this', said Paya. 'Let's swim over to the other side.'

She was one of a group of children playing crocodiles at the river's edge. The river was muddy and had a good pace to it. You couldn't see the bottom. But you could feel the thick mud with your feet if you happened to go down. The kiddies were having great fun. Who was the crocodile going to catch next?

But now, Paya had had enough. She pushed out into the deep and began to swim strongly, correcting her course against the current as she made for the opposite bank. 'Come on kids', she yelled. 'Follow me!'

But suddenly Paya found that something like the branch of a tree was coming up between her feet. There it was again; it felt weird. In a moment she found herself sitting astride a thing that seemed to have great horns. It was moving steadily downstream.

'Quick, come', she called to her friends, 'there's something underneath me. It's got horns! Quick, come and see.' But it soon swept away from underneath her.

As Paya's friends were swimming out to her, they all saw the 'thing' reappear. Yes, it did have horns and they thought they could see the brown whiskery appearance of its face. They all swam back to the longhouse wild with excitement to tell the story.

'Ah yes', said the headman, 'that was Naga the river spirit. If we treat him kindly he will send luck to us.'

But some of the longhouse folk thought the headman's reaction a very strange one. They didn't want to pay respect to Naga any more. 'We are Christians, aren't we?' they queried.

'True, we are Christians', the headman confessed, defensively. 'But a little respect to Naga will do us no harm. I suggest we make a feast of celebration. We could do with some luck right now.'

But Avit, one of the young men, was very unhappy.

'This thing we call Naga is really of the devil', he said. 'If we make a feast in honour of him it will mean that we worship him and not the Lord Jesus.'

Young Avit didn't like speaking against the headman's words but he felt strongly that this could be the beginning of backward steps right into the devil's camp.

AVIT'S CHALLENGE

When the folk gathered for church that Sunday the issue of Naga was a very live one. Some of the village elders were strongly in favour of the feast to honour Naga. 'What if he were not honoured', they argued, 'and he sent disaster upon us? We've got to be sensible and look at this thing realistically. Of course we are Christians, friends, but let's be reasonable.'

This talk made Avit feel sick and he could stand no more of it. He got to his feet and walked to the front, taking with him a picture which he intended to use. The picture was of a man standing beside the Cross of Jesus. The man had his foot on the head of a large snake. It was dead.

'The snake in this picture is like Satan', he said. 'When we became Christians we put our foot on Satan's head. We said that Jesus is our King.'

'He's right. His words are true', some faithfuls declared.

'But now, what are we trying to do?' Avit continued. 'This Naga is an evil spirit of the river. He belongs to Satan. If we honour Naga it means that we honour Satan; Satan is king. But if we say "No, we will not make this feast", it means that Jesus is ing.'

Avit let his words sink in and held his picture high. There was a deathly silence. No one moved.

'Who is it to be then?' he asked. 'Who is it that has the victory, Satan or Jesus? Whom do you say?'

The folk shuffled and coughed nervously. Avit had hit the nail on the head. Many felt ashamed. A couple of the elders were angered.

After a while, one stalwart plucked up courage. 'We want to follow Jesus', he said.

'Jesus is King', another called. 'We will not make a feast to Naga. Jesus is King.'

Avit was thrilled. He gently folded up his picture and made for his seat.

The Sunday morning service continued in its normal way and the feast to Naga was called off.

Avit left home to go to Bible School shortly after that. The picture of the man beside the Cross with his foot on the serpent's head was pinned to the longhouse wall for all to see. And Satan went back to his workshop to work on another device for deceiving these young Christians.

Guidelines

Satan's stratagems
' "All these I will give you, if you will fall down and worship me." Then Jesus said to him, "Begone, Satan! for it is written, 'You shall worship the Lord your God and him only shall you serve'." Then the devil left him...' (Matthew 4.9–10 RSV).
'Resist the devil and he will flee from you' (James 4.7b RSV).

Talkback

1 *Naga* What would make you suspicious of a Satanic stratagem behind the Naga episode? (Matthew 4.9; Leviticus 17.7; 1 Corinthians 10.20; James 4.7.)

2 *Boldness* Do you think that Avit should have just prayed and 'let the Lord do it all'? Do you see anything to emulate in his speaking out as he did? (1 Samuel 2.30b; Psalm 107.2; Acts 4.19–20; Galatians 2.11.)

3 *Vacation?* Are Christians permitted a vacation in their watchfulness against the devil's wiles? (Matthew 26.41; 1 Thessalonians 5.5–6; 1 Peter 5.8–9.)

4 *Modest life?* 'If I live a modest life and do no one any harm then folk will know that I'm a Christian'. Is this

typical of New Testament Christianity? (Mark 15.43; Acts 4.13; 9.29; 14.1–3.)

Jesus gives boldness

'When the council saw the boldness of Peter and John, and could see that they were obviously uneducated working men, they were amazed and realized what being with Jesus had done for them' (Acts 4.13 Living Bible).

TRUNK CALL

In the morning, the converts were called together and Eban, their leader, again appeared with the egg. Holding it up before us he said: 'This is my telipun (telephone). I talk to the spirit of Bungan through the spirit in this egg.

Then, with jungle knife in his right hand and the egg in his left, he walked out on to the outer verandah and commenced his swansong to Bungan. I heard his shout at the end, 'Goodbye, we're finished, we're through!'

Of Birds' Nests and Bridges . . . 23

Do you like birds'-nest soup? You've never tasted it? The Chinese people in Borneo like it and pay high prices for the birds' nests.

These nests are built by the little cave swiftlets in the various Bornean caves, and look like saucers stuck to the cave roofs. The swiftlets are amazing little birds that feed on airborne insects. They can even drink in flight, dipping down to the rivers and opening their bills with perfect precision to flick up a mouthful of water.

They make their nests mainly of the yellowish saliva from their mouths, but sometimes mix it with a little moss or vegetable matter. We sometimes see Chinese women sitting outside their shops working with tweezers extracting the moss and downy, chick feathers from the birds' nests that they have bought in the market. The nests are then turned into soup, a thickish, yellow substance, not very strong in taste but eaten as a rare delicacy.

Akin was a man who owned some of these valuable birds' nest caves in an area some distance from his own village. He knew a little about the gospel, and on one of his nest-gathering trips he decided that he would stop over in the area and seek out some of his relations and friends to tell them about Christ. This is how the gospel often spreads in Borneo, through folk telling their relations in other areas. These relationships are God's bridges over which the Gospel travels into new districts.

Akin found his relations living in a downstream long-house about eight miles from his caves. He stayed with them for Christmas and told them what he knew of the Christmas message. This whetted their appetites for more and very shortly a letter arrived at our base, sent from these people.

The letter was so lavishly couched in spiritual language that I discerned that somebody who knew something about God had helped them to write it. It was Akin. They wanted, they said, 'to know more about the all-glorious

and most high God . . .' and would we please send someone
to bring the Christian message to their pagan longhouse.

NIGHT OF DECISION

Within a couple of weeks, Pastor Yohanis and I were
canoeing our way up the twisting little river on which their
longhouse stood. Our stay with them we found to be hard
work, as some of the witchdoctors tried to forestall a
change. They stood to lose materially, and both Yohanis
and I could feel a wave of oppression creeping over our
spirits as the Satanic opposition increased. On the final
night I went out into the night air and cried to the Lord
to break this oppression and set the people free.

At this crucial meeting where all the village folk had
gathered, they spoke much among themselves. Finally, after
presenting the gospel, we asked them to come to a decision
for the night was getting late. We knew that some of Akin's
friends were just waiting for a lead from one of the village
elders before they made an open response. It soon came.

Eban, one of the witchdoctors, rose firmly to his feet and
coughed loudly to demand attention. 'My fathers, brothers
and sons', he said, 'we have heard the big news the visitors
bring . . .' and he went on to elaborate upon it. Finally he
declared, 'To me, this is good news and tonight I'm going
to become a Christian. Who's coming with me?'

He then produced from his small, bamboo tobacco container a little egg which he had secreted away there. He
said it was a rooster's egg. It was ceremonially important
in his following of the pagan cult which he said he was
about to part with. He then offered the egg around to
anyone who would take it, suggesting that in their grasping
of it they were indicating their desire to break with the
Bungan cult and follow the Christian Way. Quite a circle
of folk called for it and took it firmly in their right hands
before passing it on.

In the morning, the converts were called together and
Eban, their leader, again appeared with the egg. Holding
it up before us he said, 'This is my *telipun* (telephone). I
talk to the spirit of Bungan through the spirit in this egg.'

Then, with jungle knife in his right hand and the egg in his left he walked out on to the outer verandah and commenced his swansong to Bungan. I heard him shout at the end, 'Goodbye, we're finished; we're through.'

With that, he came inside, slipped the sacred egg into its pouch and walked with Yohanis down to the river's edge to commit it to a watery grave. We then began a short time of teaching.

The faith of Akin, the birds' nest dealer, has been rewarded as there are now four other Christian groups in that area.

I could end the story here and we might have a happy ending. But really, the introducing of folk to the Christian faith is just a beginning and not an ending. A beginning which throws big responsibilities upon us.

Herein lies a problem that perplexes me. These folk, like many others in remote areas, have had so very little teaching over the few years of their Christian life. Pitifully untaught, they cling on to the little they have had. Oh to see them growing, healthy, strong; but that would mean more Bible teachers of which there are so few.

This is the problem : is it right for us to keep on pressing in to unevangelized areas whilst folk in evangelized areas remain so untaught? What do you think is the answer?

Guidelines

Family evangelism

'(Andrew) first found his brother Simon, and said to him, "We have found the ... Christ." He brought him to Jesus ...' (John 1.41, 42a RSV).

Talkback

1 *Base things* Why do you think God so often uses unlikely people and unlikely ways and means to fulfil His purposes? (Isaiah 55.8–9; 1 Corinthians 1.27–31.)

2 *Leadership* How important do you think good leadership is to the progress of a Christian group? (Jeremiah 50.6; John 10.11–14; Ephesians 4.11–12; 1 Peter 5.1–4.)

3 *Natural gifts* Eban was a gifted village leader. Have natural gifts any place in spiritual work? (Mark 1.16–18; Acts 18.2–3; 1 Corinthians 2.14–16.)

4 *Bridges* Can you think of any 'bridges' that God has arranged for you to move across in sharing the good news with others? (John 1.41–42; 4.3–7; 35–36.)

God guides us

'In paths that they have not known I will guide them.
I will turn the darkness before them into light,
The rough places into level ground.
These are the things I will do,
and I will not forsake them' (Isaiah 42.16 RSV).

DOUBTS UNRESOLVED

If you've read Pilgrim's Progress *you will recall how Greatheart and his companion, after they had conquered Doubting Castle and killed Giant Despair, found the dungeon full of dead bodies and dead men's bones. Doubts unresolved can be disastrous . . .*

Who Shut the Lion's Mouth? . . . 24

'Oh, God', Susan cried, 'if it's true that you really did shut the lions' mouths, show me just how you could do it! Prove it to me, Lord!'

Susan had a problem. Her trouble may sound foolish to you, but it was very unsettling to her. She was a missionary Bible teacher and had walked many miles over Borneo's mountains telling the folk of a God who could meet every need. Many had come to the Lord through her witness. The Lord could meet everyone else's need. But could he meet hers? This was where the crunch came.

What was troubling her? Just this. She became bothered by a doubt as to how on earth God could possibly shut the mouths of the lions that threatened Daniel. The doubt was becoming more and more insistent, and Susan knew that if she could not have it resolved it would spawn other questions about God's power and cripple her ministry. It had hot breath.

The fact that she knew who was behind the doubt didn't help. She had taught that Satan's first appearance into the realm of man's innocence was with a question about God's integrity. She knew so much! But this. This was different.

THE TREK

The work didn't stop just because Susan had a problem. There were folk depending on her to tell them more of God's love and faithfulness. Should she tell them what was happening in her own heart—the agony of it? She couldn't.

The time soon came around for her to go away on another teaching trip. Some more hard walking was involved, over rugged mountains. She had ample time for reflection on the lengthy walks between villages. And the carriers with her sometimes lagged behind a little, so as to let Susan set the pace for the team without feeling she was being hurried. They were always considerate of her like this.

But—how could God possibly shut the mouths of those

lions? 'Come, come now', said a little voice. 'You surely can't swallow stories like that?' Susan was getting worn out. Dare she speak to someone about it? Wouldn't it sound awfully improper for a missionary to confess a thing of this nature?

'O Lord, help me', she gasped as she slid down over a rocky knoll. 'You've got to do something to help me, Lord.'

If you've read *Pilgrim's Progress* you will recall how Greatheart and his companion, after they had conquered Doubting Castle and killed Giant Despair, found the dungeon full of dead bodies and dead men's bones. Our doubts can be disastrous for us if we toy with them instead of bringing them humbly to God.

Susan walked on. The path through the jungle to the next village was over some lonely hills where people rarely went. The forest's forty shades of green lay in unspoiled profusion. Susan's track was strewn with fallen leaves and moss-covered rocks. Now and again little trickles of water furrowed the path to make it muddy and treacherous. She had to keep her eyes glued to the track. It was just as well that she did.

As she trudged forward, she saw something before her which stopped her abruptly, right in her tracks. Her next step could have been fatal. Right at her foot was a deadly cobra about 12 feet long, stretched out right across the path. Susan froze with fear, expecting the worst. But the cobra didn't move an inch. And its mouth stayed shut! Most unusual for a threatened killer snake. It did not strike or even attempt to bare its deadly fangs. She backed off quietly. The cobra then slithered off into the small bushes.

Who shut the cobra's mouth? Susan had no need to ask. Daniel's escapade was no longer a problem. She thanked God and took courage at this graphic display of His power to help people who call upon Him in times of great need. And she now helps others along the lines of the Scripture that says:

'God is faithful, and he will not let you be tempted beyond your strength, but with the temptation will also provide a way of escape, that you may be able to endure it' (1 Corinthians 10.13b RSV).

Guidelines

For good
'And we know that all things work together for good to them that love God, to them who are the called according to his purpose.' (Romans 8.28 AV).

Talkback

1 *Doubts* Is it only weak Christians who have problems with their faith? (Job 21; Psalm 73; 1 Corinthians 10.12–13.)

2 *Resolved* Can you think of any disciples who had doubts about Christ? How were their doubts resolved? What can we learn from Christ's dealings with them? (Matthew 11.2–6; John 20.24–29.)

3 *Uplook* When troubled by a doubt, would it be better to fill our minds with the *certainties* of God's love and faithfulness rather than dwell on the problem itself? (Deuteronomy 7.9; 1 Samuel 2.2–4; Psalm 27; 89.1–2; Hebrews 7.25; 10.23; Revelation 12.11.)

4 *Fellow-feeling* Missionaries in lonely places are especially susceptible to doubts regarding God's faithfulness and credibility. In what ways do you think you could be a friend indeed to such folk? (Acts 20.35; Romans 15.1; Hebrews 13.3; Matthew 18.19–20.)

God feels it too

'In all their affliction he was afflicted, and he personally saved them. In his love and pity he redeemed them and lifted them up and carried them through all the years' (Isaiah 63.9 Living Bible).

NIGHTMARE

'I have had two dreams that have terrified me ...

'In the first dream, my father had just taken the head of a man. He was in the jungle. When I went up to him he tried to hide the head by putting it down between a pile of logs. I parted the logs and put my hand down inside to get the head. But when I did, a barking deer sprang out of the hole and dug its teeth deep into my arm and wouldn't let go ...'

Man against Demon ... 25

Lisut moved sullenly, following the riverside track from his longhouse to our little hut. Then he stopped, thought for a moment and came up the steps, his stooping shoulders and furrowed brow shouting to us that something was very wrong.

He had cropped his hair as a sign of distress and deep humiliation.

Under normal circumstances Lisut would have been a happy man. He had keen yet kindly eyes. He seemed a sincere Christian who could look quite objectively at his dilemma.

'It's no use', he said, 'I can't, I can't.' With that he bent his head over on to the table at which I was sitting and began to cry like a child as he told God about the demon which had been troubling him. He had been trying to sleep when suddenly he had been rudely awakened by something that had shaken his body violently and pulled his hair. Things like this had happened so often before.

He had looked around the room for the intruder, but as usual there was nothing to be seen. 'It's no use. I can't beat this thing', he wept.

Lisut's father had been a powerful witchdoctor when he was alive. He was also a headhunter. But when he died it seems that one of the demons that had possessed him came to trouble Lisut. Lisut had never been vexed in this way previously, neither had he any aptitude or desire to follow in the steps of his father.

But now the demon was in full pursuit and Lisut had been almost driven to distraction by these relentless intrusions into what might have been a serene and well-ordered life. Demons cannot bear the prospect of disembodiment and will do anything to hold a position of acknowledgment, worship and obeisance.

Lisut had already been down to the town for treatment. Coastal practitioners had treated him as a mental case and after a long period of freedom from symptoms, he had been sent back home with a clean sheet. This was puzzling. All the time Lisut was away from home he seemed to have little or no trouble with the demon. But while he was away the last time, his wife had committed suicide! This was a terrible shock to Lisut; the devil had indeed been active during his absence.

THE DEMONIC INTRUDER

It was not long after Lisut's return to his longhouse that the demon began pestering him again. For fear that he might become violent and do damage to life or property during these satanic intrusions, the folk gathered all the jungle knives, weeding hooks, etc. from his room so that the demon would virtually have no iron weapon to use against them. Lisut heartily agreed with this, for he was of a gentle nature.

But then, one day folk heard wild yells coming from his room and rushed to see what all the commotion was about. Lisut's younger brother, Jau, lay on the floor before them holding his throat. A distraught Lisut stood beside him. They learned that Lisut had tried to choke his brother who was almost blind and could not see or easily move away from impending danger. In his distress Jau had called, 'It's the demon; Lord Jesus, Lord Jesus, save me!' Lisut's grip on his throat slowly relaxed.

Yet the Christians of the village harboured no fear of Lisut as a person. They knew only too well what was behind the trouble and they also knew from Jau's experience that there was a greater power that could make the demon let go.

Lisut bent over the table in an attitude of utter frustration and impotence. As he sobbed out his heart about this recent visit of the demon to his room, I thought that it was time that we did something more than pray from a distance.

Waking my two friends who were having a midday rest, I suggested that we all go along to have a good look at Lisut's room and pray there. I remembered the story of an Indian pastor who, when faced with a similar case, had insisted on almost ransacking the room of a demon-influenced person in order to search out any hidden causes. Was there some hidden satanic medicine, charm stone or magic device secluded there? If so, the demon could not be dislodged until everything of satanic significance was removed.

Lisut's room was dark and dingy and for a moment we could see little but a light cane mat on the floor and the coals of a smouldering fire. We immediately made a parting in the roof shingles to let a little sunshine through. Pastor Alang placed a board against the door to keep it open while we cast our eyes around the smoke-blackened walls of the room.

'Lisut, are you really sure that you have nothing in this room that the demon might cherish—stones, shells, fetishes, little wooden gods, leaves, anything? Are you really sure?' Lisut was sure.

'Well, what about your daughter, and your brother, Jau, who also live here? Have they got anything? Even the smallest thing is enough to give the demon leverage against you.'

'Nothing, nothing at all', declared Lisut with a lift of his hands. We believed him.

'But before we all pray', said Pastor Lassa, the senior one among us, 'I'd like to ask you a question, Lisut. Is there anything about which you are afraid, something that is giving you a very heavy heart?'

We were startled by the immediacy of Lisut's reply. 'Yes, there is', he flashed back. 'I've had two dreams that have terrified me and I cannot get them out of my mind.'

THE TWO DREAMS
'In the first dream my father had just taken the head of a man. He was in the jungle. When I went up to him he tried to hide the head by putting it down between a pile of logs. I parted the logs and put my hand down inside to get the head. But when I did, a barking deer sprang out of the hole and dug its teeth deep into my arm and wouldn't let go. I screamed in pain and released the head.'

Lisut paused and swallowed, his eyes glued to the floor. He then continued.

'In the second dream I was sitting down idly throwing stones into a hole which I was trying to fill. I kept on throwing and throwing but the hole would not fill. Then I took a big stone and threw it. This one went into the hole and then suddenly flew back and hit me hard in the stomach. I have had a sore stomach ever since then. Both of these dreams are a great heaviness to me. I can't get them out of my mind.'

We all sat speechless for a moment, contemplating the implications of Lisut's dreams. Then Pastor Lassa spoke.

'It seems to me, Lisut, that these two frightening dreams are the devil's work to shatter you with the weight of your past sins. Lisut, you can beat this. You say you are fully trusting Jesus. Then you must see that Jesus has absorbed *all* your sins into His own body and paid the full penalty in *His* death on the cross. Are you going to bear them still or believe that Jesus has borne them for you?'

Lassa went on to elaborate how that Jesus had not only dealt with our sin but also our guilt, and no more could the devil beat a trusting soul over the head with the stick of impending judgment. Jesus has taken up the sinner's case.

'When Satan presses you again like this, refer him to Jesus. Praise Jesus Christ for His victory over Satan and bid Satan and his demons be gone, in Jesus' Name.'

Suddenly the truth dawned upon Lisut. He smiled and raised his hands in recognition. 'I see it, I see it!' he said. He then repeated back all that Lassa had said, anxious to take up the name of Jesus as his defence.

Then Lassa stood up and placing his hands upon Lisut's head, announced that he was now going to pray, asking God for complete deliverance for this man Lisut. 'And I want you all to do the same.' Everyone prayed aloud, 'We want Lisut to be delivered in Jesus' Name.'

I saw Lisut several times after that, asking him how things were going. One day he came up to our hut to bring us some fruit that he had picked. He was delighted to be given free enough range to go out by himself and get it. He had had no more trouble with the demon, but his stomach was still sore.

Guidelines

The warfare
'... we are not fighting against people made of flesh and blood, but against persons without bodies—the evil rulers of the unseen world ... and against huge numbers of wicked spirits in the spirit world' (Ephesians 6.12 Living Bible).

The Victor
'The reason the Son of God appeared was to destroy the works of the devil' (1 John 3.8b RSV).

Talkback

1   *Dreams*   What would you teach new tribal Christians regarding the relevance or otherwise of dreams? (Jeremiah 23.26–29; Psalm 119.11, 50, 67, 133; 2 Timothy 3.15–17.)

2   *Slaves*   'Animistic heathen are not only in error, they are slaves', says a writer. In what terms does the Bible describe this slavery or bondage? (John 8.34; Romans 6.16; 2 Timothy 2.24–26; Hebrews 2.14–15; 2 Peter 2.19.)

3   *Prayer*   Can demons be prayed out of a person? How big a factor is prayer in the deliverance of demon-influenced people? (Mark 9.28–29; Luke 18.1–8; James 5.16.)

4   *Command*   Jesus commanded demons to come out. Have we that prerogative? (Luke 4.36; 10.17–20; Acts 16.16–18.)

5   *Cooperation*   How important is the cooperation of the demon-influenced person and his family in the deliverance from evil powers? (John 5.6; 1 Corinthians 5.6–7; 2 Corinthians 6.14–18; Ephesians 5.11.)

God our refuge

'Who dares accuse us whom God has chosen for his own?
Will God? No! He is the one who has forgiven us ...

'Who then will condemn us? Will Christ? *No!* For he is
the one who died for us ... overwhelming victory is ours
through Christ who loved us enough to die for us' (Romans
8.33, 34, 37 Living Bible).

IN THE WEST

*Yakob . . . found the constant wearing of suit and necktie
a little irksome, and table etiquette a thing to be watched
with considerable care. The inside spoon was for the dessert
and the knife at the left for the bread and butter! And . . .
'was it one lump of sugar, Yakob, or two?' . . .*

A Shot When Needed . . . 26

Yakob is a Bornean of great spiritual stature who was
invited to Australia by a Mission group to inform the folk
there about the young church in Borneo.

He had many adjustments to make on arrival in that
land, but found that he was cushioned into them by his
prior knowledge of the ways of so many missionaries. He
found the constant wearing of suit and necktie a little
irksome, and table etiquette a thing to be watched with
considerable care. The inside spoon was for the dessert and
the knife at the left for the bread and butter! And ... 'was
it one lump of sugar, Yakob, or two?'

He was taken to see 'our harbour bridge' and 'the tallest
building in the South.' He did appreciate the kindness and
enjoy seeing the sights, but when would he see his beloved
mountains again and hear the hoot of the hornbill and the
rush of the highland streams?

He couldn't help noticing the affluence; the host of
gimmicks and gadgetry and the worship of chrome and
steel. And the people in a hurry! Why the rat race? What
did they all do and where did they all go at night?

Young Christians in Borneo who have been to Western
colleges to study speak enthusiastically of the things that
have made them glad to know their fellow-Christians 'over
there'—the warmth they felt in Christian homes and the
folk who accepted them simply as they were without trying
to force Western patterns upon them or presuppose Western
attitudes. This is not to say that they did not suffer culture
shock nor sometimes cry into their pillows at night over the
times they felt misunderstood or humiliated by some of our
abrupt Western ways.

The amenable and patient Yakob took it all in his stride
and soon became a seasoned traveller with many friends in
many places. Although he had only a limited knowledge
of English, folk loved him for his ability to communicate
by smile, sign and the diligent use of the few words at his
command. These he honed up and used with great skill.

Something that Yakob said in Australia about the Bornean church has stuck in my mind. I will tell you about it.

In the course of his visits to the capital cities Yakob was taken to a large private home where he was to meet some students and others in a kind of Borneo forum. He was with others out at the front.

After he'd given a picture of the Bornean church, it was question time. The silence was quickly broken :

'Sir', said a student, 'you have been telling us all about the church in Borneo and how the Christian message has had such a remarkable impact. But tell me, have you thought much about the uncertainties of the Asian situation as things are happening these days. How do you think your church will stand, should Communism for instance push in upon your country and the church has to suffer? How will the faith go then?'

Yakob thought for a moment. He was never quick to answer at any time and now he pondered over the question. Yes, he thought, here's a man who's been thinking.

'You ask me how our church will fare in a crisis situation', he replied. 'Is our faith strong enough to meet such an eventuality? May I answer that by telling you of an experience I had recently in another of your capital cities?

'I was staying in the home of a Christian doctor who asked me if I'd like to go along with him to a hospital and observe a surgical operation that day. Being unused to such things I had qualms at first, as I pictured the patient writhing before the surgeon's knife and having to be held down by strong men! But following the doctor's gentle assurance I went along.

'When we arrived at the operating theatre, everyone was dressed in white robes. Things looked immaculately clean. The whole set-up savoured to me of another world.

'Then the assistants brought in the man for the operation. To my surprise he was in no way agitated, but lay there quite at peace with everything.

'The surgeon beckoned me to come closer. He then picked up a little knife and made a long incision. That knife sank deeply into the man's flesh, but he didn't even wince. He just lay there asleep, in a state of seeming bliss as if he was enjoying the whole experience. And the surgeon went on to complete his task without the slightest bother.

'Now, I ask you, why didn't that man scream? How could he face that crisis with such equanimity? You know the answer. Because of the pain-killer, the anaesthetic given him by the doctor at the time of his need.

'How will the Bornean church go when it has to face trial and perhaps persecution? Maybe it hasn't the resources now because it doesn't need them. But I believe our Lord's words, that at the time of special need He will give the special strength.'

Back here in Borneo, Yakob often uses this experience to teach the church and to comfort people who are afraid. He sees that its significance is becoming increasingly relevant, for here we have a young church facing an uncertain future, but with the very certain hope that the Lord who helps people in deep need will help them, as He said : 'When you go through deep waters and great trouble, I will be with you. When you go through rivers of difficulty, you will not drown! When you walk through the fire of oppression, you will not be burned up ... For I am the Lord your God, your Saviour ...' (Isaiah 43.2–3 Living Bible).

Guidelines

Power for the weak
' "My grace is all you need; for my power is strongest when you are weak." I am most happy, then, to be proud of my weaknesses, in order to feel the protection of Christ's power over me' (2 Corinthians 12.9 TEV).

Talkback

1 *Contact* What can you do to contact students from overseas in your country and make them welcome in your

7—OWTTJ * *

circle? (Luke 14.23; John 1.41–42; 2 Timothy 1.16–17.)

2 *Good soldiers* In what ways can you help prepare these students to become good soldiers of Jesus Christ in the non-Christian contexts to which many of them will return? (2 Timothy 2.1–4; Matthew 16.24–25; John 8.31–32; 15.8.)

3 *Normal Christian* What is the New Testament pattern of the 'normal' Christian life: one of trial and conflict? Or one of peace and joy? Are the two mutually exclusive? (Luke 9.57–62; John 14.27; 16.33; 1 Peter 4.12–16.)

4 *Crises* In what ways can we expect God to help us in times of crisis? (Psalm 23.4; Isaiah 43.2–4; 58.10–12; 1 Corinthians 10.12–13.)

Remind your people . . .

'Remind your people of these great facts, and command them in the name of the Lord not to argue over unimportant things . . . Work hard so that God can say to you, "Well done" ' (2 Timothy 2.14a–15a Living Bible).

PRAYER ANYWHERE

'Sir, will you invite us to your house?'
    'But, why should I invite you to my house?'
    'Because, sir, we want to pray with you.'
    'Well, what's wrong with praying right here outside my office?'
    And pray they did . . .

Hand on My Shoulder . . . 27

It made us glow at Mission headquarters the other day
to receive a very special kind of letter. It began in this
way :

'Rejoice, for you have won another brother and sister
for the Lord through your persistent prayers. The Lord
listened to your prayers and has done away with the old
Yosup and made him born again as a new Yosup, your
real brother in Jesus Christ. Truly, truly I am born again
and all my past self is now dead.' How was Yosup
converted?

Yosup had done well for himself. Headmaster of a high
school at 25, a charming young wife, a nice home perched
right on top of a hill that commanded a magnificent view
of surrounding villages, an airfield and a fertile valley.

Yosup had been taught the Christian way as a lad, but
after leaving home he began mixing with the wrong crowd
and eventually came to calling himself an atheist. At the
high school where he now was he had told the students
very straightly that there was no God and that for them
to bring their Bibles to school would be treated by him as
an act of provocation that he would not stand for.

He would fly down to the town as often as possible,
where he was popular with his drinking partners. He also
bathed in the honorifics associated with his position and felt
very comfortable amidst the revelry of Vanity Fair.

But God's time came for Yosup when a spiritual awakening occurred among the students of his high school. It
went on for several days before he began to feel its
imminence in the extra meetings the students were having,
coupled with the exuberant singing and long sessions of
audible, excited prayer that resounded through the meeting
room like a sweeping wind.

Then, Yosup was visited by a band of students.

'Sir, will you invite us to your house?' their leader asked.

'But why should I invite you to my house?'

'Because, sir, we want to pray with you.'

'Well, what's wrong with praying right here outside my office?'

And pray they did. The students wept and poured out their hearts to God for their headmaster. This touched Yosup deeply but he did not want to admit it. Nor did he want to tell the boys that he'd had a feeling that evening that in some way or other God was going to make the area a holy place. After their time together, the students shook hands with Yosup and went back to their meeting.

Yosup now felt bereft and bewildered. He wanted God but he didn't want Him. 'Oh, God', he cried, 'if you really have something for me, please send those students back here right now.'

Within a few minutes the students were back and Yosup began to realize that God really did have something for him. 'They explained the way of salvation to me with such carefulness and clarity', said Yosup as he described it later. 'I felt as though I was the student and they were my professors. They pleaded with me to repent of my sins and turn to the Lord. And on that day, I did.'

Visions

Very soon after this, Yosup met the Lord in a night vision in which his sins were revealed to him one by one, and a great number of tears were shed as he agreed with the Lord that these were indeed heinous and things for which he was truly sorry. 'The Lord was very kind to me', said Yosup. 'It seemed as though my head was on His lap and His hand was on my shoulder as I made my confession before Him. It lasted for about four hours. By morning, my pillow was wet with tears, but such joy filled my heart.'

Yosup was not a man with a flair for special revelations, and yet the Lord had another confirming vision for him. He was shown a crimson, hard-covered book like an encyclopedia. It was opened at a clean, white page on which were the words: 'Yosup Jun Kalang was a great sinner and has now turned to the Lord.' The date was added. Being a man acquainted with rolls and registers,

Yosup remarked how comforting it was to have his name listed on the Lord's register of births.

At his first attendance at a meeting with the students and other teachers, Yosup found it hard to pray. He was shy and somewhat inhibited. Seeing his difficulty the students immediately began crying to the Lord for him right in the meeting, 'Lord, loose his tongue; Lord, please make him free. If Jesus makes us free, we are free indeed.' Feeling for him, another teacher came and stood beside him and helped Yosup openly to confess the Lord in prayer before the students.

'And now', said Yosup's teacher friend, 'you go home and open your Bible. Read what God draws your eyes to. God is wanting to speak to you from His word.'

Back home, Yosup rummaged around in a cupboard for an old English Bible. It was wrapped in paper and had been carefully put away. He opened it, not knowing what was to come. His eyes fell on Romans 8 verse 1 : 'There is therefore now no condemnation for those who are in Christ Jesus.' The sun began to shine brightly for him, and the Bible that he had despised became a thrilling book which he could not put down.

Gradually, as he gained spiritual muscle, the Lord revealed things that had to be dealt with. One of the first of these related to his possession of a valuable, Javanese charm stone that he had tucked away. It was said to have great protective powers. The medicine man who sold it to him for $25 assured him that no harm could come to the person who possessed it. It also had magic power to turn people to the owner's advantage. You could never lose a court case if you took it with you.

Yosup had trusted much in the power of this stone, especially to protect him from the power of the person who, it was said, had poisoned his father. It had to go. He took two boys along with him and although the stone was supposed to be unburnable, it quickly disintegrated before the flames that day. All three of them stood there in front of the fire and praised God who had given them such boldness in testimony to Jesus' power over this evil thing.

There were also folk whom he had to seek out to make restitution. 'I wanted to be wholly clean', said Yosup, 'that there might be nothing between me and the Lord.' This involved a quest for Markus, the parliamentary representative for the district. On Markus' return from a trip abroad, Yosup waited for him at the airstrip until the other welcoming dignitaries had gone, so that he could have a quiet word with him to ask forgiveness for a wrong. This greatly humbled Markus, who was also touched by the Lord at this time.

THE REMARRIAGE

Then, Yosup and his wife Merta, who had never been far from the Lord all along, decided that they would like to be married in a Christian manner. Their marriage previously had been merely witnessed by a village headman, a normal practice among non-Christians. 'We must now make our marriage confession before the Lord', said Yosup, 'and ask His blessing.'

But a problem arose in the preparations for the wedding feast. Not enough cake could be found. The folk could only rustle up enough for a few. 'Well', thought Yosup, 'if the Lord could multiply loaves and fishes, surely He can bless the cake and make it sufficient for all.' They prayed.

The 'wedding day' was one of great happiness for them as they affirmed their love for the Lord. A good company gathered to witness their union as 'newly-weds in Christ' and Markus the parliamentarian gave the 'wedding address'. But what about the cake? Everyone had enough and there was some to spare.

FINAL EXAMS

Final exams were approaching for the older students. Much time normally spent in cramming had been spent by them in ministry and prayer. Yosup was concerned lest this mean failure in their exams. Already the authorities were aware of the spiritual activities in the school and would rightly ask questions, should there be a lot of casualties.

Yosup prayed, asking God to overrule for His own Name's sake. His heart was greatly warmed at that time by the reading of a certain portion of Scripture. It told of the apostle Paul's lengthy preaching which seemed not unrelated to the death of a young man, Eutychus, who fell asleep and dropped from his place on the window ledge. When others had given up hope for him, Paul embraced him saying : 'Do not be alarmed, for his life is in him.'

From this Yosup believed that all would be well with his students in their exams. They would not 'die' as a result of the working for the Lord, but 'live.'

God did overrule. The school gained the highest percentage of successes in the state, and each one of the student preachers received a first grade pass. And Yosup knew that 'None who have faith in God will ever be disgraced for trusting him.' (Psalm 25.3a Living Bible).

Guidelines

God first
'. . . trust the Lord completely; don't ever trust yourself. In everything you do, put God first, and he will direct you and crown your efforts with success' (Proverbs 3.5–6 Living Bible).

Talkback

1 *Witness* Can you think of any Scriptural precedents of children speaking for God to their elders? (1 Samuel 3.16–18; 2 Kings 5.2–5; Luke 2.46–49.)
2 *The mouth* Do you agree with these students regarding the importance of confessing Christ with the mouth? (Psalm 107.2; Romans 10.8–10.)
3 *Wisdom* How would you advise the students about witnessing for Christ in time normally given to study? (1 Corinthians 14.20, 40; Titus 2.6–8; James 1.5–6.)
4 *Scriptures* What counsel would you give these folk

regarding a. the use of the Scriptures for particular guidance, and b. general usage for daily strength and growth?
(Deuteronomy 8.3; Joshua 1.8; Psalm 119.11; Colossians
3.16; 2 Timothy 2.14–15.)

Learn, teach, sing . . .

'Remember what Christ taught and let his words enrich
your lives and make you wise; teach them to each other
and sing them out . . .' (Colossians 3.16 Living Bible).

BUFFALO BUYER WITH A BIBLE

... Another man in town for the regatta was Lukas. He was a buffalo dealer who mixed the telling of the good news with his buffalo-buying trips. He would bring the animals back to his interior village where they would be slaughtered and their meat flown out in large trays to this regatta town. Lukas had been deeply touched by the recent revival ...

Look Who's in Town ... 28

28 Look Who's in Town

An interesting thing about visiting a Borneo township is the folk you meet from so many tribes and races. I've just returned from a visit to a semi-coastal town where a biennial regatta was held. A sightseer couldn't have wished for a better bird's eye view of the various inhabitants of the whole area. Everybody who was somebody was there, together with his friends and poor relations. Let me tell you about some of the events and people involved in this working trip to this town.

In keeping with the speciality of the occasion we had been given permission to erect a round-timbered bookstall right in the town's central square in the hum of things. Besides being a bookstall, it was a haven of care where folk could come and talk about anything. A special diesel-electric generator had been brought in to strengthen the town's sagging power reserves. Our bookstall was the last to be wired up, but I was thankful that we would have lights right from the word go.

There were crowds in town. What an array of bright sarongs and ultra shirts! Folk swarmed around our bookstall like flies round a honey pot. Bornean young people love books. Books are windows on to the big, new world before them, and the fact that ours were Christian ones made no difference. They have no inhibitions about religion. Religion is a part of every man's scheme of things. They had many questions they wanted answered about the Christian faith.

Which books were the most popular? Books about people, books that warmed the heart, that told how others had found the answer to life's questions. And there were the immaculately-presented modern versions of the New Testament that sold briskly.

'And where are you from?' I asked a young fellow standing beside me. He was dressed in tee-shirt and jeans and looked like one of the leather-jacket group at home; a little of the rebel in him and a touch of the cynic, but out to get the best from life. He had a beaming smile.

'I'm a Land Dyak', he replied, describing his tribal background. 'I just happen to be working up this way. Got a job on an oil rig.'

'Are you a Christian?' I asked further.

'Me? No, as a matter of fact I'm open to anything. That's why I've come to look at your books.' We had a good talk together, after which he bought a New Testament and dissolved back into the crowd. We prayed that he'd swell the numbers of those who come to Christ on the strength of the little book that is 'living and active.'

Next to our bookstall was a useful neighbour; an arts-and-crafts stall that carried a variety of blowpipes, beads, jungle knives and raffia baskets. You could also buy a honey bear there or a grey gibbon if you liked; a yellow-billed myna or a cormorant; all of which gradually disappeared as time went on.

We now have a church building in this town, a sturdy one built from the savings of churches in the area with a little outside help. It was erected by a hearty team of New Zealanders who came out as 'Men with a Mission'. The church now has two pastors; one for the tribal congregation and another who tends a growing Chinese flock.

FOLK IN TOWN

As in most Borneo towns, the Chinese are the main inhabitants. They have great facility for business and always show an interest in a deal. Many of their shops are open from early morning till last thing at night in the hope of gathering in the last few cents from a willing straggler. Some of them follow the Buddhist faith. A number are ancestor worshippers who cast a reverent eye to the framed photos of their forebears, enshrined in their shops and homes. But many are showing interest in the Christian faith these days, as our pastor will tell you. His church has been growing steadily.

Although the traditional habitat of the tribesfolk is the

hinterland, many of them have now come to the towns for work or study. At this particular time crowds of tribesfolk were in town for the regatta; come to take part in the boat races; to see the festivity, the displays, the visiting dignitaries and the bazaars that were stuffed to overflowing for the occasion.

You can distinguish the older tribesfolk from the town dwellers by their poorer dress and rugged demeanour that speaks of battle with the elements, with sickness and poverty and the stress of a pagan environment that has shown no mercy. Though many of them have now become Christians they will never outlive some of the marks of a sinister past.

Many tribal young people take their places with others of the towns in responsible positions as teachers, administrators, office workers, nurses. Some are soldiers, a few policemen. Added to these are the throng of tribal students who are not one whit behind their town counterparts in intelligence and ability. Many of these young people are now turning to Christ.

One particular tribal family caught my eye as they sauntered past our bookstall; I knew they were strangers here. Seeing them brought memories of the piercing crows of fighting cocks on a longhouse verandah, of a basket full of rejected charms; of the night we introduced them and their folk to the Christian faith in a village some 200 miles away. What brought them here?

'We've moved,' said the man, mopping his forehead and edging towards some shade. 'Our old farmland was finished and we've just got permission from the chief here to take up some better land.' He was exuberant. They looked tired, however, after a day of tramping around the bazaar area looking for somewhere to sleep the night.

It wouldn't surprise me if they soon have a Christian group around them in their new location. A little bit of the good news can work wonders. We trust it will, as 240,000 of this family's kinsfolk still do not understand why Christ came.

FOOD IN FIVE LANGUAGES

Another man in town for the regatta was Lukas. He was a buffalo dealer who mixed the telling of the good news with his buffalo-buying trips. He would bring the animals back to his interior village where they would be slaughtered and their meat flown out in large trays to the regatta town. Lukas had been deeply touched by the recent revival and had been given a gift of healing through prayer. Many folk had been drawn to Christ through his ministries, for he taught as well as prayed.

Lukas preached very humbly in one of our special meetings. I can't recall his theme but I do remember what happened at the end. He said we would have prayer for the sick. 'If you've anything wrong with you and would like to trust the Lord Jesus for healing, just place your hand over the sick spot as we pray', he said.

Many folk responded; none seemed shy about their ailments. I raised my hand to my head as I thought of my hay fever. Then Lukas turned to me : 'I'll now ask the missionary to pray for us all.' I hoped I'd misheard the signal, but I hadn't. Lukas repeated : 'The missionary will now pray for us.' How grateful I was for the attitude of prayer and the atmosphere of simple faith that pervaded that meeting.

Lukas is a man of many parts. After the meeting he wanted help in moving a tethered deer of his from its feeding spot to a place inside the church gate, away from menacing dogs. The deer was stubborn. Eventually, Lukas had to shed his very best dignity and apply a stout shoulder to the deer's rear while I pulled.

'Now', said Lukas, rubbing his hands as if the job had been well done, 'let's find an eating place and have a meal.' He insisted on paying for it, saying how good the Lord had been to him of late.

Have you ever heard a sermon in five languages? Well then, you must come to Borneo. Folk flocked to our church on the Sunday morning. Sapling bearers had been used to extend the church roof over the rows of extra seating that had been brought in for our regatta-time services. Three parliamentarians sat up the front, one of whom was Markus who had been asked to preach on this morning.

He attached the mini-mike around his neck, opened his big Bible and began : 'Today, I want to speak to Christians. Let us hear what the Bible says about the Holy Spirit's likeness to the dove, the bird that is gentle, that is loving and that grieves over its beloved.'

Straight from the revival area, Markus then laid it on the line what it means to be possessed, loved and grieved over by the Holy Spirit. This he did in five languages, using the national language, Malay, as his main medium and digressing into three tribal languages and English to make sure that all present got the burden of his message.

A student choir from the high school then sang two pieces to challenge and stir our hearts. I don't think that any of us missed the point of God's word to us that morning. Markus himself was rejoicing in the Holy Spirit's work among his own people. He said that God had worked among them in the nick of time and allayed his fears that the church might fall into the hands of clever but worldly-wise men.

DEPARTURE

The next morning I watched the helicopters lifting the visiting VIPs off the cement pad and away back to their polished desks and fan-cooled verandahs. How pleasant and cordial the handshakes of well-wishers. All would have been so orderly had it not been for the ugliness of a pagan funeral procession that cut right in close to the field of ceremony.

The coffin was carried on a beflagged, open truck and preceded by hooded mourners. Frantic relations wailed out their grief as the procession moved with haunting inevitability to the graveyard. I thought, what an inappropriate time for a funeral; what an ill-fitting farewell gesture to high-ranking officialdom! But then, couldn't it have been a gentle reminder for us all that life's pageant does come to an end; a terrifying one for those outside of Christ; everlasting joy and gladness for those who hear and receive His invitation to life.

But 'how are they to hear without a preacher? And how can men preach unless they are sent? As it is written, "How beautiful are the feet of those who preach good news!"' (Romans 10.14-15 RSV).

Guidelines

Commission
'And the master said to the servant, "Go out to the highways and hedges, and compel people to come in, that my house may be filled"' (Luke 14.23 RSV).

Talkback

1 *Multi-racial* Some Asian churches are multi-racial. What things do you think a missionary would particularly have to watch in working with a multi-racial church? (Romans 15.1; 1 Corinthians 9.19-23; 10.31-33.)

2 *Build?* What do you think should be the first aim of a missionary in a town setup : to get a church building up or a Christian fellowship going? (Isaiah 66.1-2; Acts 17.24; 1 Corinthians 6.19-20.)

3 *Function* What should be the function of a missionary ministering in a church situation : to act as captain or as coach? (Matthew 28.20; 1 Corinthians 12.7-11; Ephesians 4.11-16; Colossians 3.16-17; 2 Timothy 2.1-2.)

4 *Debtor* What did Paul mean when he said : 'I am debtor...' (Romans 1.14-15). To whom was he in debt? What did he feel in debt about and what did it cost him to discharge it? (2 Kings 4.7; Acts 20.17-27; 2 Corinthians 11.23-29.)

What Paul felt

'I am debtor ...

'I am ready ...

'... I am not ashamed of the gospel of Christ : for it is the power of God unto salvation to every one that believeth' (Romans 1.14, 15, 16 AV).

THE DRY FIELD

*'My father has a sore problem. His field is dry and parched
and it will yield no padi without water. Yet, he has a
spring not far away. Oh, tall bamboos, my father asks
your help in getting the water to his dry field ...'*

29 The Bamboo that Agreed

(Adapted from an Asian parable.)

Kimbing the *padi* farmer looked on his dry field. It was cracked by the hot sun, and furrowed by dusty buffalo tracks. Kimbing had good land if he could only get water to it. He threw back his grass hat and scratched his head. The sweat trickled down his leathery face. It was hot.

'What can I do?' he asked himself. 'I've got the water in my spring. It is good water. It makes things grow. It turns them green. But how to get it on to my farm; that is my problem.' He brushed a fly from his nose and squinted as he looked through the shimmering heat to his yellow, sun-baked soil.

This was the season for planting. Kimbing's family trusted him to get *padi* from his little, square plot. But the water. How?

Kimbing looked at his bamboo fence. How well it had stood up to the buffetings of his buffaloes as they nudged it and scraped their dusty hides.

'The bamboos!' declared Kimbing as a useful thought flashed through his mind. 'They have served me well. Perhaps they can serve me again?'

KIMBING SEEKS HELP

The next day, Kimbing sent his son to ask help of the tall bamboos that lived in the forest bordering his farm.

'My father has sent me to ask your help', said the boy as he stood before the cluster of towering bamboos. They looked so stately and superior in their forest home.

'My father has a sore problem. His field is dry and parched and it will yield no *padi* without water. Yet, he has a spring not far away. Oh, tall bamboos, my father asks your help in getting the water to his dry field.'

The bamboos creaked and groaned as they jostled one another, their slender heads peering down from a great height. They were talking over the farmer's request.

Eventually, one bamboo giant spoke :

'I will help', he said.

'But you will have to be chopped down and it will hurt', said the son. 'Think well how you will answer.'

'I have', said the tall bamboo. 'I will help.'

'But, you will have to be removed from your shady spot here in the jungle.'

'I know it', said the bamboo. 'Your father wants help, doesn't he?'

'But, bamboo, you will have to be shorn of all your fine foliage. All your leaves will have to go.'

'Let it be', the bamboo continued. 'Your family will die without *padi*. I can channel the water that makes the *padi* grow.'

'But that is not all, O brave bamboo. Not only will you have to be cut down and removed from your shady place. Not only will you have to be shorn of your leaves. But the knots inside you will have to be removed so that the water can flow. Have you thought of that?'

At this, all the bamboos seemed to sigh and creak. The son remembered that he was now asking the hardest thing of all. He turned again to the tall bamboo who now spoke.

'I have considered the request of your father. I will go with you. What more?'

And so the tall bamboo was removed from his place, shorn of his finery and deprived of the hard knots. He was put in his new position between the spring and the dry field. And the water began to flow on to the thirsty land of Kimbing's *padi* farm.

Kimbing smiled as the *padi* seedlings began to sprout and then came into head. His family would live and not die. He was grateful for the tall bamboo that had agreed.

> Just a channel, full of blessing,
>   To the thirsty hearts around;
> To tell out Thy full salvation
>   All Thy loving message sound.

Emptied that Thou shouldest fill me
  A clean vessel in Thine hand;
With no power but as Thou givest
  Graciously with each command.

M. E. Maxwell

'Love through me, Love of God.'

ONE THING MORE

What of the church now? Is it alive and well, you may ask? Please do not think I am being facetious in using the above heading. I use it with intention because it sums up what is very much a burden of my heart at this time.

As you will have gathered from the last couple of chapters, there is a reviving work going on in several areas. And one could easily spoil that work by giving it unwise publicity. I do not intend to do that. Yet, we cannot help but say a big 'Thank you, Lord' for what He's doing. It's thrilling to see some of the churches full to capacity, die-hard sinners praising the Lord and folk telling others out of pure joy. And in student groups, fellowships of government workers and meetings of school children, there is a new touch of Life.

But now, many of these new believers are asking : Where do we go from here? How do we get to know Jesus better? How do we grow in the faith? Teach us about the Holy Spirit. And there are the problems : What do we do about the visions that have been popping up among us? And the folk with dreams to tell, do we hear them? And the man who says he has the gift of discerning other people's sins? Now these questions are not just the offshoot of the spiritual awakening, they are always with us to some extent, but more than ever now. How are we going to teach these brethren?

Yesterday, I heard of a young student who rejected the pagan religion of his parents. Then he found that he had no religion at all. This also proved very irksome, for he longed for a God to pray to and worship.

While sitting in his classroom he began to doodle with his pen and drew a picture of a man. Its neatness impressed him and so he added further titivations to it which made it more appealing. Then he said to himself : 'This picture is good. This man can be my god. I will pray to him and worship him.' This he did. He worshipped the picture that he had drawn. It gave him a little satisfaction, but yet didn't fill the vacuum. He recently heard the good news of Christ and accepted Him, and is now living in the truth of a true God and Saviour.

I tell you this to emphasize that if men cannot have the truth when they seek it, the devil will give them something to fill the gap. And this has relevance, I believe, to these new Christians seeking teaching. Hunger unmet becomes a great pain that can drive spiritually hungry folk to seek out the purveyors of revelations, dreams and cheap spiritual highs. The outcome is disastrous, unless they can be rescued by God's truth brought to them by faithful men.

Teach them

What made the lame man of Acts chapter 3 go walking and leaping and praising God? It was the touch of Jesus' power. But he walked and leapt his way into the temple. Any man who has been touched by Jesus needs instruction in how to use his quickened faculties. But, most important of all, he needs to know how to walk the long stretch—the walk of faith in company with Jesus.

It is easy to question: 'Why then aren't these new believers being taught and built up in the Word of God?' We might well reply: What Word of God? Only *one* of the tribes here has a full Bible in its own language as yet. Four other tribes have New Testaments and others a few books of the New Testament in their own language. And who is to teach them when the Bible teachers are so few? And how do we get to them, for they live 'way over the mountains?

These are some of the problems we have to work at in giving these new or revived Christians the whole counsel of God. I fear that in all the talk of church-planting these days, it is assumed that to plant churches is all we have to do. Now, we don't dispute the importance of planting churches. We have been involved in it. But there is the possibility that in our passion to get more churches started (and perhaps the status attached to it), we leave an awful trail of impoverished, depressed and debilitated converts behind us.

Paul's desire was that he might 'present every man mature in Christ' (Colossians 1.28 RSV). And the only way he could do this was by giving them the Word of God, teaching them night and day 'with all humility and with tears' (Acts 20.19 RSV). And also, we might add, living among them as a *learner* as well as a teacher. We busy, busy people often have no time to sit and learn from those among whom we move. But Paul was different, and he got different results. He wrote of his desire to visit the Roman Christians '. . . that we may be *mutually encouraged by each other's faith,* both yours and mine' (Romans 1.12 RSV).

To sum up then, Jesus taught us in Luke 11.24–26 that you cannot leave a man's soul empty. It is presumptuous to tell a person to empty his heart of the old without giving the wherewithal to fill it with the new. Jesus speaks of the results of such neglect in terms of an evil spirit returning to the emptied heart with seven worse devils . . . 'and the last state of that man becomes worse than the first.'

The emptied, repentant heart must be *filled* with the Word 'which is able to build you up . . .' (Acts 20.32 RSV). Paul prayed for the Colossians '. . . that you may be *filled* with the knowledge of his will . . .' (Colossians 1.9 RSV), and exhorted them to 'let the Word of Christ *dwell in you richly*' (Colossians 3.16 RSV).

We missionaries here have the privilege of working alongside a young, indigenous church whose guests we are. There is much to do in the area of church planting, for this land of Borneo is still largely pagan. And there is a backlog of teaching to do in the churches, among the students, etc, and in training those who can 'teach others also.'

That's the task ahead, as far as I can see. And we trust the Lord to carry us through, so that those who are and will be walking and leaping with the pure joy of Christ will go on to praise Him in fruitful lives, as responsible members of the body of Christ.

> Spirit of God, ev'ry man's heart is lonely,
> Watching and waiting and hungry until,
> Spirit of God, man longs that you only

Fulfil the earth, bring it to birth,
And blow where you will.
Blow, blow, blow till I be
But breath of the Spirit blowing in me.

From the song : *Spirit of God*, sung by
Sister Miriam Therese Winter

BOOKS READ OR REFERRED TO

Customs and Culture, Eugene A. Nida (Harper & Brothers), 1954

The Living Christ and Dying Heathenism, Joh. Warneck (Baker Book House), 1954

What of the Unevangelized? J. Oswald Sanders (OMF), 1966

Bridges of God, Donald A. McGavran (World Dominion Press), 1957

Give up your small ambitions, Michael Griffiths (IVP), 1970

Latin American Theology, C. Peter Wagner (William B. Eerdmans), 1970

Roaring Lion, Robert Peterson (OMF), 1968

Sarawak, 1839–1963, Joan Rawlins (MacMillan and Co.), 1965

The Birds of Borneo, Bertram E. Smythies (Oliver and Boyd), 1960

Webster's Collegiate Dictionary (McGraw Hill & Co)

Information on Sarawak from the Borneo Literature Bureau.

Versions of the Bible used :

The Living Bible (Coverdale House Publishers)

Good News for Modern Man (TEV) (William Collins)

The New Testament in Modern English by J. B. Phillips (William Collins)

The Revised Standard Version (RSV) (Division of Christian Education, National Council of Churches of Christ, USA)

Other books by Ken Nightingale

TRIBE IN TRANSIT
Fascinating glimpses into the lives of the primitive nomadic
Penan people, and how they are responding to Christ and
serving Him. (Photographs) 15p

HEADHUNTER'S DAUGHTER
Lipang also knew the pagan days. Although never
trained in Bible School, she was much used as
witness and counsellor. Helpful background information.
(Photographs) 10p

THE SNAKE THAT LOST ITS HEAD
40 stories for children, approximately 8–15 years. Illustrated
with line drawings. 35p